PEOPLE WHO GARDEN
IN GLASS HOUSES

or have their own glassed-in windowsills
can have a little bit of summer blooming all
year round. And with the help of *The Greenhouse
Gardener* you too can experience the joys of
flowering greenery, whether the sun is shining
or the snow is piled all about. Everything you
need to know is included, from getting the right
equipment to the proper spot to build your own
plant haven; from month by month instructions
about what to plant, what to force, working
with seeds and cuttings, watering, fertilizing,
combating insect pests, and what greenhouse
maintenance is necessary to a complete listing of
the care and habits of 134 different flowering
plants which are suited for greenhouse growth.

So why hesitate. Join the ranks of the gardening
elite and be the first in your apartment house
to say, "The calla-lilies are in bloom," when
everyone else is saying, "Baby, it's cold outside."

THE GREENHOUSE GARDENER

SIGNET Books of Special Interest

THE GREENHOUSE GARDENER

Elvin McDonald

A completely revised, updated,
and expanded version of
The Flowering Greenhouse Day by Day

LINE DRAWINGS BY KATHLEEN BOURKE

A SIGNET BOOK
NEW AMERICAN LIBRARY
TIMES MIRROR

NAL BOOKS ARE ALSO AVAILABLE AT DISCOUNTS
IN BULK QUANTITY FOR INDUSTRIAL OR
SALES-PROMOTIONAL USE. FOR DETAILS, WRITE TO
PREMIUM MARKETING DIVISION, NEW AMERICAN LIBRARY, INC.,
1301 AVENUE OF THE AMERICAS,
NEW YORK, NEW YORK 10019.

Library of Congress Catalog Card Number: 66-16904

Published by arrangement with the author

SIGNET TRADEMARK REG. U.S. PAT. OFF. AND FOREIGN COUNTRIES
REGISTERED TRADEMARK—MARCA REGISTRADA.
HECHO EN CHICAGO, U.S.A.

SIGNET, SIGNET CLASSICS, MENTOR, PLUME AND MERIDIAN BOOKS
are published by The New American Library, Inc.,
1301 Avenue of the Americas, New York, New York 10019

First Signet Printing, May, 1976

4 5 6 7 8 9

PRINTED IN THE UNITED STATES OF AMERICA

Contents

List of Illustrations

LINE DRAWINGS

Figure

Prologue: *Greenhouse Gardening On a Time Budget*

The Greenhouse Gardener is a natural outgrowth of *The Flowering Greenhouse Day by Day,* a book I wrote in 1965 and which was published the following year. Its content was based on some twenty years of gardening in my own greenhouses, the first a sun-heated pit I dug and constructed on my parents' Oklahoma ranch before I was ten years old. By 1965 I had progressed to a 10 x 20 glass-to-the-ground greenhouse which was attached to my home in suburban Kansas City. I was Editor of *Flower and Garden* magazine and had already written my first two books *(Miniature Plants for Home and Greenhouse* and *The World Book of House Plants).* In addition, I was director of a large church music program, had gone back to music school, and was being prepared for the Metropolitan Opera Auditions. At home I was a husband, the father of three young children, and the chief groundskeeper of a huge lawn and a seemingly endless flower border which had enough crabgrass in it to make me wild-eyed and sweaty every summer weekend. Life was hectic and full of stresses, but I was happy, in part because of the quiet times I spent in my greenhouse.

As conceived originally, *The Flowering Greenhouse Day by Day* was intended as a handbook to guide in the transformation of an empty, bare-benched greenhouse into a vision of thriving, flowering plants. I was torn between being told by the news media that there was a national overabundance of leisure time and the reality of having less and less of it myself. The books I had read about home greenhouse gardening either told me more about engineering and construction than I needed to know, or else they emphasized the culture of individual plants without giving a clear-cut, overall program for how to run a greenhouse.

With all of this in mind, I decided to do some market research on my own, but with the cooperation of Lord and

Burnham, pioneers in the field of prefabricated home green-houses. They agreed to provide me with a mailing list of five hundred customers, both new and old, in a random mix, who were widespread geographically. I then prepared a lengthy questionnaire which went into the mails with a brief covering form letter. I explained why I needed the answers, but offered nothing in return for the considerable amount of time it would take to fill out the questionnaire. The response by return mail was nearly overwhelming, and in particular to the question, "From your experience, is there one main problem that has been troublesome in oper-ating your home greenhouse?" A majority reported that the greatest problem was lack of time, and the general tone of all was, "Stop the world, I want to spend an hour or two in my greenhouse."

What I suspected, but did not know for sure until com-pletion of my survey, was that home greenhouse gardeners are among the busiest people on earth. More than half of the questionnaires returned were from professional men and women—doctors, editors, lawyers, ministers, and teachers.

Lack of time was not the only major problem expressed in the questionnaires. A doctor in Kansas said he should have built his 10 x 14 greenhouse twice as large. Pest control was a frequent concern; a rancher's wife in Montana ex-pressed it this way, "I always have to cope with aphids and other contaminations brought in by well-meaning friends who donate plants." A well-known musician from Connecti-cut wrote, "Baby-sitters are easier to find than plant-sitters."

Fay Scott Payne, to whom I dedicated the original book as well as this revision, wrote that in most of the eighteen to twenty years of home greenhouse gardening she had been totally disorganized. Her letter continued, "Over the years I have changed the arrangement of my greenhouse inside and out four times. When I first had the greenhouse I let it run me. Then I ran it for my convenience. Now we have reached an understanding: we work for and with each other."

In every questionnaire I found useful information, and in many there were delightful anecdotes that stemmed from the pleasures of having a home greenhouse. A surprising number confessed that they had been failures as greenhouse gardeners, but were now hoping to find the keys to success in my book.

In *The Greenhouse Gardener* I have tried to retain the best of *The Flowering Greenhouse Day by Day,* at the same time revising and updating where appropriate. All of the photographs are new, but the charming and informative line drawings by Kathleen Bourke are from the original work. I have added a portfolio of photographs which show the wide range of available prefabricated greenhouses, from window and portable units priced at under one hundred dollars to large, permanent installations which are relatively costly. It is important to note that when you need additional living space for dining or just plain relaxing, a prefabricated greenhouse is today's biggest bargain in terms of cost per square foot. The greatest plant cultural changes since 1965 have occurred in the area of pest control and growing mediums, both of which I have completely updated, along with the Lists for Ready Reference (see Appendix). In addition, many plants cut for budget reasons from the galleys of the original Chapter 13 have been reinstated.

Preparing the manuscript for *The Greenhouse Gardener* has been an unusually pleasant activity for me because I am in the midst of constructing my fifth greenhouse, and the first I will have had for several years. It is in fact larger than any of the previous, and in my mind the space is filled already with healthy, flowering plants. I foresee no bugs, no problems, and I will have unlimited time to relax and enjoy the greenhouse. A gardener's hope springs eternal.

ELVIN McDONALD

January, 1976
New York City

Introduction: *How to Realize Your Greenhouse Dreams*

We are brought together as reader and author because of a common interest: greenhouse gardening. My premise is that either you have a home greenhouse now, or that you will have in the future, and that your desire is to have lots of flowers. Whether you visualize a flowering greenhouse every day of the year, or only from fall to spring, this book can be your guide.

The first twelve chapters suggest greenhouse work for each weekend of every month, but remember at the outset that all of this work does not have to be done on such a rigid schedule. For example, you can do anything suggested for March at any time in February, or in April, with approximately the same results.

FIRST DECISIONS ABOUT GREENHOUSE BUILDING

My first greenhouse, built by me before I was even a teenager, was a simple pit in the ground with secondhand window sash as the covering. It proved one thing—this was a way to garden without all the limitations of four definite seasons. My next greenhouse, a slightly larger lean-to, was constructed of scrap lumber left over from a house my father was building. It was glazed on the south side with double-strength glass, and on the ends and top with plastic-covered screen wire. Now, nearly twenty years later, my parents still enjoy this greenhouse, with replacement of the plastic-covered wire required every two or three years.

In 1961 I progressed to a prefabricated greenhouse that I built in a few days' time with the help of relatives, friends, and neighbors—not that the job was that complicated, but rather so interesting that everyone wanted to assist. We

1   This 3 x 5 plastic-covered greenhouse costs less than $100 and can be assembled in 30 minutes without a nail, screw or tool. Casaplanta

erected the framework, installed the glass, the benches, and flooring, but called in local craftsmen to do the concrete foundation and to install the wiring, plumbing, and heating equipment.

HOW MUCH DOES A GREENHOUSE COST?

Cost varies, of course, from practically nothing for a makeshift lean-to over a basement window, to several thou-sand dollars for a structure say 20 x 30 feet with an a-tached potting shed and garden house. Chances are you will find the greenhouse of your dreams at some point between these two extremes.

Plastic has done more than any other single factor to

2 *Strong, translucent panels of fiberglass form the roof and walls of this 10 x 10 free-standing greenhouse which comes with a 14-inch, thermostatically controlled fan to help maintain ideal temperature.* WHEELING CORRUGATED COMPANY

put a greenhouse into the realm of possibility for anyone. I have an acquaintance who enjoys a polyethylene-covered greenhouse 10 x 10 x 8 that cost initially only forty dollars. Now even those who rent or lease their homes can usually erect a small prefabricated greenhouse or a simple plastic-covered one on a portable foundation such as redwood timbers. At moving time the structure can be disassembled and transported to the new location.

HOW LARGE A GREENHOUSE?

While cost is an important factor, you will want to think at the same time about how large a greenhouse you really need. I progressed upward from 4 x 8, to 6 x 9, to 10 x 20 feet. I know now that it is easier to keep the large greenhouse neat because there is more room to space out plants properly, but there is also more maintenance work.

How much time does it take to look after a home greenhouse? Naturally you have to take into consideration the size and the kind of plants cultivated. My 10 x 20, which houses a variety of more or less common plants and a few rare kinds, does nicely on one to four hours every Saturday morning, plus an average of 15 minutes daily. This takes care of watering, transplanting, propagating, and cleanup.

ROOFTOP AND HIGH-RISE TERRACE GREENHOUSES

If you live in an apartment building and want a greenhouse, the landlord may be willing to give permission. On rooftops the main concerns are weight and moisture leakage. Where weight is a problem, a plastic-covered greenhouse may be the solution; in addition, you may need to use only lightweight plastic pots and soil-less growing mediums. In recent years many high-rise terraces have been enclosed with either prefabricated or custom greenhouses. Where permitted, this makes what is largely wasted space —owing to air pollution and street noise—a useful area for living and gardening in all seasons.

3 Fiberglass, whether plain or corrugated, is virtually shatter-proof, oblivious to hailstorms, and diffuses sunlight so that shade- and sun-loving plants can be cultivated alongside each other. No additional shading materials are required, even in midsummer.
PETER REIMULLER

WINDOW GREENHOUSES

If a conventional greenhouse is out of the question for you, either economically or for lack of a place to put it, consider a window greenhouse. Several models are available, two of which are shown in Photographs 10 and 11. These come complete, ready to install over a house or an apartment window.

4 This prefabricated greenhouse has a sturdy redwood frame with heat-conserving double walls of plastic. The dead air space between the two layers of plastic reduces heating costs up to 50 per cent. VEGETABLE FACTORY

The growing space inside a window greenhouse receives more light or sun than the room from which it extends, and there will also be more humidity. One of these makes an excellent place to grow a collection of small foliage and flowering plants, as well as to start seeds of vegetables, herbs, and flowers for planting outdoors in warm weather. If the window greenhouse is shaded in winter, and therefore on the cold side, it may be used for wintering-over hardy bonsai trees and shrubs. And a cool, mostly shaded window greenhouse can be ideal for forcing spring bulbs such as crocus, tulips, hyacinths, and miniature daffodils into winter-flowering plants. Gift plants in full bloom, such as primrose, cineraria, chrysanthemum, azalea, and cyclamen will also last longer in a window greenhouse than they will in the hot, dry atmosphere of the average house or apartment.

You can use a window greenhouse in a window that faces north, east, south, or west. Which will be best depends on the climate where you live, the time of year, and the kind of gardening you want to do in your window greenhouse.

If you live in the North, you can enjoy your window greenhouse during the fall, winter, and early spring months if it is placed in a sunny east, south, or west window. You can also use it in a north-facing window, but you may find it best to remove the plants on cold, windy nights when the temperature hovers around zero. From late spring through summer, while the sun is hottest, your window greenhouse will do best in a north or east window, or in a tree- or shrub-shaded south or west window. In sunny, warm, winter climates, such as Florida, south Texas, and southern Cali-

5   *When a greenhouse like the one above is run on the cool side during the heating season, with a nighttime minimum temperature of 40 degrees F., vegetables like lettuce, carrots, scallions, and radishes can be grown and harvested all winter.* VEGETABLE FACTORY

fornia, a north or east window may be better all year, unless you want to grow only desert cacti and other succulents. By the same token, during hottest summer weather no matter where you live, your window greenhouse will be best in summer only for cacti and succulents if it receives midday sun.

At any season you begin to use your window greenhouse, it is a good idea to place a thermometer inside among the plants. Check it at various times of the day and at night so that you will have an idea of the highs and lows. Most houseplants do well in a temperature range of 60 to 80 degrees.

What about supplementary winter heat? Where winter temperatures dip to zero, it is advisable to remove the

6 *Strong, transparent plastic and redwood forms this prefabricated, geodesic dome greenhouse which requires no permanent foundation. It measures 14 feet in diameter, is 8 feet high; also available in a lean-to model for attaching to a house or other building.* REDWOOD DOMES

7   This all glass and aluminum lean-to prefabricated greenhouse can be erected in a day's time after the permanent foundation is completed. LORD & BURNHAM

plants to a warmer place indoors until the sun is shining outdoors to make the window greenhouse once again comfortable for your plants. You can also use an inexpensive portable soil-heating cable to help your plants' roots stay cozier during coldest weather. One other tip: if you have placed a thermometer inside your window greenhouse and readings on it are on the chilly side for the plants you are growing, try using a small circulating fan inside the room near the window greenhouse. This will constantly exchange the colder air in the greenhouse with warmer air from the adjoining room.

MOST GREENHOUSES NEED SUN

Before you start looking at catalogs and plans for home greenhouses, consider whether you have a good place on your property for such a structure. Except in the deep South and sunny Southwest, greenhouses need to be located where they have full sun for at least a half day in the fall and winter. Filtered sun provided by tall, deciduous (no leaves during freezing weather) shade trees is fine for spring and summer.

I have known a number of home greenhouse gardeners in the South who have located greenhouses on the east, even north sides, of dwellings, with bright open space all around, and they have had much success. They find that shading and cooling during warm months is much less a problem than for greenhouses that face south or west.

Home greenhouses are designed in two basic styles, even-span and lean-to. The even-span has two sides, two ends, and a roof. The lean-to has one side, two ends, and a roof. The even-span can be attached to a building, thus eliminating the need for one end. All lean-to greenhouses are attached to some other structure. When placed on the south of a building, a lean-to is much less costly to heat in the winter and makes a delightful addition to a living area. A lean-to can also be placed in the ell of a building, thus eliminating the need for one end, or in the U-shape formed by two wings of a house, with no ends required.

Before you buy a prefabricated greenhouse, or start a do-it-yourself project, check local building restrictions. If you live in the country, this may not be necessary, but in any organized urban or suburban area, you will probably need a building permit. Certain communities may have by-laws in homeowner associations that permit no buildings on a lot except the dwelling. This means that you will have to attach your greenhouse to the house as I did. A friend in Des Moines who wanted a detached greenhouse met a similar local restriction by attaching it to the house by means of a grape arbor. Now the breezeway between the greenhouse and house is refreshing with a bricked floor, a display of potted plants in summer, and dappled shade cast by the grapevines.

GREENHOUSE FOUNDATIONS

Once you decide on a greenhouse and place your order, the manufacturer will make available to you the foundation specifications. Except in mild climates where freezing seldom occurs, greenhouses require foundations that extend below the local frost line. These are usually made of poured concrete reinforced by steel rods. There are basically two types of foundations. One comes approximately to ground level, with the greenhouse having glass or plastic to the ground. The other has a foundation or wall of wood, stone, brick, or concrete blocks that extends about 3 to 4 feet aboveground, meeting the glass or plastic at that point. It is this second type that is better in the far North, but glass to the ground is practical northward through USDA plant hardiness Zone Seven (lows of zero to ten degrees).

If you live on rented or leased land and want a greenhouse, but do not want to invest in a concrete foundation, investigate the possibility of using redwood, cypress, or cedar timbers onto which the greenhouse sills will be bolted. If

8   *This curved-eave, even-span prefabricated greenhouse of glass and aluminum is attached to a garage. Stone, of a type used elsewhere on the property, forms the base. It has been sited so that deciduous trees give cooling shade in summer, but allow ample sun to reach the greenhouse in winter.* J. A. NEARING COMPANY

9 *This curved-eave, even-span prefabricated greenhouse is free-standing, situated at the back of a suburban yard with a terrace and furniture for outdoor living.* TEXAS GREENHOUSE COMPANY

you do this in a severely cold climate, use polyethylene covering, not glass, as the heaving caused by alternate freezing and thawing could break the glass. However, this method works well even with glass in mild climates, provided that the site is solid and level.

PLUMBING AND ELECTRICITY

To be really enjoyable, every home greenhouse needs ample plumbing. I could not get along without hot and cold water, with a mixing faucet to which I attach a 25-foot length of dark green hose. This means that even on the coldest morning of the year I can give pleasantly warm water to tropicals.

Have the greenhouse wired for electricity. I use a 100-watt light bulb every 4 feet along the peak of my greenhouse roof. This gives plenty of illumination for enjoyment and work in the greenhouse at night. In addition, I have a plug-in desk lamp at the potting bench to help me in transplanting seedlings.

GREENHOUSE HEATING

How you will heat your greenhouse is determined largely by what is most practical locally. I use natural gas with the warm air circulated by a fan. If this stove fails, there are infrared heat lamps ready to place into the roof sockets, and a small electric heater with circulating fan. If electricity goes out, we have two gas line connections in the greenhouse so that small heaters that do not require electric power to operate can be utilized. These precautions may seem too elaborate, but we have had to resort to both, and at times when the weather was so cold that I could have lost every plant.

As a general rule, gas or oil heat is the most economical in the North, with electricity best in the South where very little heat is necessary except in the middle of winter. All gas or oil units need to be properly vented, otherwise plants may be damaged. Many small greenhouses, if attached to a dwelling, can be warmed by extending the existing heating system.

GREENHOUSE SHADING AND COOLING

While heating may seem all-important, shading and cooling are just as vital to success. Even while the outside temperature hovers at zero on a sunny winter day, solar heat may warm the greenhouse to the point that the ventilators open for brief periods through the midday period. From midspring until early fall, most home greenhouses require some kind of shading material to keep the sun from overheating the plants.

Shading may be as simple as planting grapevines around

the greenhouse, or more complicated as whitewashing, using lath frames, roll-up bamboo curtains, or a plastic shading cloth like Lumite saran. The effect you desire is important here. Some people want the utilitarian and do not care how it looks. Others demand a good looking shade material. (See Chapter 5 for a complete discussion of greenhouse shading methods.)

Heating and cooling controls for the home greenhouse can be manually operated, but the wisest investment you can possibly make is in automatic equipment. Be sure that thermostats for all units are located where the sun will not strike them.

Besides shading, cooling, and heating, a properly moist atmosphere is another key to successful greenhouse gardening. Automatic humidifying equipment for most prefabricated greenhouses is available at extra cost. A humidifier is a necessity if you plan to grow tropicals like orchids, philodendrons, and gesneriads, but a boon for all kinds of plants, except possibly desert cacti.

In the absence of a humidifier, the best way to add moisture to the air is to wet down the walks, walls, and floors every morning, except in cold, cloudy weather, and again at noontime if possible.

GREENHOUSE FLOORS AND BENCHES

A clean greenhouse floor is one big help in keeping a greenhouse nice to look at. I have a floor of patio blocks laid on a bed of sand tamped firm. Here and there the blocks have been removed to create pockets for special plants. Bricks and flagstones also make good greenhouse floors. Poured concrete is less desirable because it does not have the moisture-holding qualities of the other materials.

After you have completed the greenhouse, with flooring, plumbing, wiring, and heating in place, you will need benches—display areas for plants—and a place for potting. My first greenhouse was nearly all bench space with barely a turn around left for me. My second consisted of about half bench area at waist height, and the balance in a slightly raised ground bed for tall plants, and a walkway. My present arrangement is similar, except there is space for a comfortable garden chair where I take a break occasionally and enjoy the plants all around.

Greenhouse benches may be made of rot-resistant woods such as cedar, cypress, or redwood, or you may choose corrugated or plain asbestos cement, or fiberglass. You want a material that will not rot or become unsightly after years of use. Benches need drainage holes so that excess moisture can escape. My own are made of redwood, 6 inches deep, about 3 feet wide, with an inch of space between each of the 1 x 6 boards in the bottom. Some of these are left open so that air circulation is free. In other sections I have lined the bench with heavy-duty polyethylene, cut a few drainage holes in it, then filled with a good soil mixture so that plants grow directly in the bench. It is in such an area that I have installed a thermostatically controlled heating cable to help in propagating plants from seeds and cuttings.

Shelves of beveled-edge, plate glass will add prime growing space along the upper walls of your greenhouse. Trained vines and hanging baskets help complete the picture.

If possible, locate your potting bench in an adjoining room where space is not as valuable as in the greenhouse. In addition, this assures a neater greenhouse with more plants. If you have to pot inside the greenhouse proper, organize an attractive work center with containers for soil-mixture ingredients, space for labels, stakes, tying materials, a pair of hand shears, and a pencil with small clipboard to make notes.

COOL OR WARM?

The first decision to make about the operation of your greenhouse is the minimum nighttime temperature you will maintain in cold weather. A cool house is usually kept at 45 to 55 degrees F. at night, with a rise of 10 to 15 degrees in the daytime. A moderate to warm house varies from a 55- to 70-degree minimum nighttime temperature.

Fortunately, there are cool spots in most warm houses where cool-loving plants can be grown. And even in a cool house, there may be one place that is warm enough for a few tropicals. After a while you will know the general boundaries of these little climates so that they can be used to advantage. With the thermostat set in my greenhouse at a 55-degree minimum, I find that nighttime temperatures range in the winter from 50 to 65 degrees. Within the same 10 x 20 greenhouse I grow plants with such widely varied needs as cinerarias, chrysanthemums, fuchsias, calendulas, schizanthus, orchids, gesneriads, begonias, geraniums, amaryllis, beloperone, calamondin, coleus, crossandras, gloxinias, and petunias. In one warm corner tomatoes thrive and bear all winter.

SEVEN STEPS TO A FLOWERING GREENHOUSE

(1) Invest in all automatic equipment for ventilation, heating, and cooling. Use a mixing faucet for hot and cold water. Place a temperature alarm somewhere in your home

10   Where budget or space does not allow a full-scale greenhouse, a window unit like this one may be installed. It costs less than $100 and can be used to cultivate a variety of small plants such as the collection of miniature orchids shown. SURE CROP, INC.

where you or a member of your family is most likely to hear it at any hour of the day or night.

(2) Install enough lights to provide plenty of illumination so that when you want to, you can put in an hour or two in the greenhouse before going to work in the morning, or at night. This enables you to keep up and avoids saving everything for the weekend—when it may turn out that you cannot possibly be in the greenhouse for a sufficient time to do the work necessary.

(3) Limit your plant collection to a few kinds well grown. Get over the urge to collect. Commonplace plants can be beautiful when they are grown well and thoughtfully displayed. The more you diversify, the greater will be the problems of culture, pests, and disease.

(4) Grow as many carefree perennial greenhouse plants as you can. Annuals that require sowing and transplanting several times a year take a lion's share of time. On the other hand, some of the most colorful of all greenhouse plants are annuals—cinerarias, for example. Maybe you should grow ten dependable perennial plants and devote the time saved to two or three annuals that yield big dividends in floral display. The flowering greenhouse day by day depends on a selection of plants long-in-flower. Strictly seasonal bloomers—anemones, for example—will occupy a relatively small amount of total space if blooms every day of the year are to be realized.

(5) Use commercially prepared, pasteurized potting soil. In the long run this saves lots of time and trouble. I obtain 2-bushel bags of a well-known planter mix that gives good results for practically all permanent plants in my greenhouse.

(6) If your time schedule is short, and there is more to be done in the greenhouse than you can possibly accomplish, learn to decide what is most important and what can wait. If, for example, plants need feeding and pest control, you will be wise to take care. of the pest control at once, tend to feeding the first chance later. And if you have time only for watering, but cannot take care of feeding or pest control for several days, you may be better off if you discard a plant infested with mealybugs; this requires almost no time, only a decision, but if you dash off, and do not get back for several days, your pest problems may have multiplied until you cannot possibly throw out every infested plant. Another way to spot check pests quickly is to keep

11 *This full-size window greenhouse has doors which open to the inside to facilitate access to the plants. This model costs less than $100.* CASAPLANTA

a battery-powered sprayer filled and ready to use with pre-mixed pesticide. I also use a similar sprayer unit for misting my plants once a week with water to which I have added Ra-Pid-Gro, a foliar fertilizer, mixed according to the manufacturer's directions. These two sprayer units allow quick pest control and feeding when I have no time for more elaborate spraying, fumigation, or adding nutrients directly to the soil.

(7) Develop a schedule of when to do what; this planning is the answer to a well-ordered greenhouse filled with thriving, flowering plants. Keep a clipboard with paper and pencil on your potting bench so that planting notes and good ideas will not be lost or forgotten.

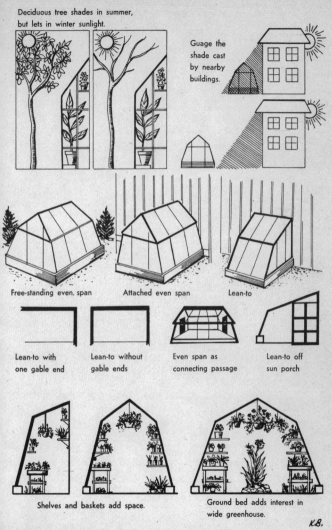

Deciduous tree shades in summer, but lets in winter sunlight.

Guage the shade cast by nearby buildings.

Free-standing even. span

Attached even span

Lean-to

Lean-to with one gable end

Lean-to without gable ends

Even span as connecting passage

Lean-to off sun porch

Shelves and baskets add space.

Ground bed adds interest in wide greenhouse.

K.B.

FIGURE 1   *Home greenhouse styles, sites and floor plans.*

1. *January*

As you work at your potting bench this month, pausing to catch the fragrance of freesias, paperwhites, and those first hyacinths, you will know that a greenhouse is one of life's greatest pleasures. January in my greenhouse brings the discovery of still more buds pushing up from amaryllis that bloomed in November, a pot of gold when crocus 'Canary Bird' blooms, and the unmatched beauty of a rose bud reaching skyward. Toward the end of the month there will be azaleas, bougainvillea 'Barbara Karst,' and a camellia joining the cyclamen in a display of Schiaparelli pink, but for relief from this shocking color, there will be wands of daffodils mixing companionably with sky-blue ixias, and the species gloxinia, *Sinningia eumorpha,* covered with creamy slipper flowers.

My greenhouse is a place of retreat in January. After the hurried activities of the holidays, I take special pleasure in a really thorough inspection of every plant. I remove all spent leaves and discard any failing plants. Inevitably this work is neglected in December, so I always plan to spend part of New Year's Day in the greenhouse. When order is restored, I settle down at my potting bench with the new seed catalogs. My practice is to place orders for seeds, plants, bulbs, and supplies twice yearly, once in January or early February, and again in August or September.

January can be a month of glorious bloom in the home greenhouse, and while you enjoy this bounty, straighten up, plan, and order. When the myriad activities of February and March arrive, you will be ready for the planting, all of your planning well in hand for the year.

If yours is a severely cold climate with rough winter storms, check the greenhouse heating system daily. If heat should be lost, and the temperature drops below freezing, raise it slowly, about 5 degrees per hour, and mist foliage frequently until the usual temperature has been reached. This procedure will save plants that might otherwise be lost. Install a battery-powered temperature alarm in a part of your residence where someone is likely to hear it at any time of day or night. If you have an alarm system already, check it out at least once every week all winter.

In the short, often cloudy days of January, keep the nighttime temperature the same, even in severely cold weather. Raising it will promote soft growth. Keep dying leaves, decaying flowers, and other debris picked up. At intervals of 6 to 8 feet along your greenhouse walkways, place a small plastic wastebasket. Spaced closely, this means that no matter where you are working in the greenhouse, you can put debris where it belongs without taking more than a step or two. Instead of feeding biweekly in January, reduce to one good feeding, or apply two at half-strength.

Water plants in the morning, if possible, so that excess moisture can dry off the foliage, and evaporate before nightfall. Keeping the soil of potted plants "evenly moist" requires much less frequent watering in January than in April.

FLUORESCENT LIGHTS INCREASE
GROWING SPACE

After January orders are in the mail, look ahead to all the seeds, bulbs, and cuttings you will be starting in February and March. You may need to add some fluorescent light units to give additional growing space.

The most common set-up is a standard industrial preheat fixture with two 48-inch, 40-watt tubes (one Cool White, one Warm White) and reflector suspended about 18 inches above the surface of a bench or table on which potted plants are placed. As the sole source of light, the lamps need to be burned 14 to 16 hours out of every twenty-four. As a supplement to natural light, fluorescents may be burned from 4 P.M. to 10 P.M. daily in fall and winter, and for longer periods on cloudy, dark days.

Fluorescent fixtures offer an excellent way to make underbench areas productive. In my greenhouse this has not been necessary since glass extends to the foundation at ground level, but several growers I know have been successful in nearly doubling total space. For convenience, install mobile

12 *One of life's great pleasures is to walk into a home green-house like this one when snow covers the ground outdoors. Flower-ing plants shown include hyacinths, cyclamen, Rieger begonias, geraniums, cinerarias, fuchsias, double petunias, gloxinias, browallia, and heliotrope.* LORD & BURNHAM

Under-bench space becomes prime growing area with fluorescent light above and soil-heating cable in sand beneath the pots.

Timer turns lights on and off automatically.

Above: Folding aluminum table with fluorescent light makes excellent propagating area. Below, left: Fluorescent unit used for supplementary light in greenhouse; right: incandescent light encourages petunia blooms in winter.

K. B.

FIGURE 2 *Fluorescent how-to for the home greenhouse.*

planter boxes of redwood lined with polyethylene and mounted on rollers. These can be moved out to get a full view of the plants and to take care of them—then rolled back quickly and easily under the lights. One *Under Glass* reader in Wisconsin reports winter bloom from geraniums growing under Gro-Lux fluorescent tubes beneath a greenhouse bench.

I grow plants under the benches of my greenhouse, and even though fluorescent light has not been needed, at times I use an electric soil-heating cable in the sand on which the pots rest. In the dead of winter the cable provides sufficient warmth to keep leaves and flowers coming the way I want them to.

In spring I use four two-tube fluorescent units in my basement to start flats of seeds. The basement temperature ranges from 68 to 72 degrees. About mid-March I begin to transfer seedlings to the greenhouse in an area where nighttime temperatures stay from 50 to 55, rising up to 75 in the daytime. An Indiana grower writes that in the winter he moves plants to his basement under fluorescent lights after they finish blooming in the greenhouse. A correspondent in Maine suggests using a fluorescent-lighted basement garden in the spring for starting tuberous begonias, gloxinias, and primrose seedlings when the greenhouse is crowded.

In summer I use my basement garden for starting seeds that need coolness. When days are torrid outdoors, impossible for cyclamen, cineraria, and calceolaria, I get good germination in the basement under fluorescents. One July, I started a flat of snapdragons for winter blooms in the greenhouse. They stayed on the cool basement floor six weeks with one 20-watt fluorescent tube lowered to 3 inches above the tops of the plants and burned 16 hours out of every 24. This set-up produced the sturdiest crop of snapdragon seedlings I have ever grown.

One reason for installing fluorescent fixtures is to supplement natural light during the short days of late fall and on through winter until spring is on the scene with plenty of sunny weather. A grower in Rhode Island writes of using two units, each equipped with two 40-watt Gro-Lux fluorescent tubes, and burned 14 to 16 hours daily, for starting seedlings and for flowering gloxinias all year. A correspondent in Virginia uses three similar fixtures with

Gro-Lux tubes burned 4 to 5 hours in the evening over the benches in fall and winter to promote flowering.

There is still another reason for going the fluorescent way. Many of us hope to grow a little of everything—and this materializes into a lot of everything. While we want them all, they will not necessarily thrive in the same greenhouse. Some like it cold and others need a junglelike atmosphere. If you face this predicament, grow tropicals under fluorescent lights in a warm basement or other room of your home, and maintain your greenhouse in winter for plants that need a cool, airy, sunny situation.

First Weekend of January. Feed plants in active growth with a half-strength solution. Feed bougainvillea twice this month with a 0-14-14 or 2-12-12 fertilizer. It will do wonders for flower production. While you make the rounds, check every plant closely for signs of insects and diseases. One slip in pest control now can mean a battle later—a few mealybugs on the leaf undersides of an innocent-looking coleus, for example, can cause a lot of trouble.

Tulips, daffodils, and other spring-flowering bulbs you have potted up for forcing should have a good root system now. Bring a few pots into the greenhouse.

Pay a call on your local garden center. You may find a supply of plump, healthy gloxinia tubers on hand, and a shipment of hybrid amaryllis. Planted now, these will give you a welcome flower show in March and April.

Second Weekend of January. This is the usual time in the month for taking cuttings, repotting, and dividing. However, if your January days are cold and cloudy, put off such activity until later. Bring in more pots of hardy bulbs for forcing. Now, while the days are short, check to be sure the glass is clean. Dirty panes reduce the amount of light. To keep down the growth of algae inside, use a household detergent to wash all greenhouse parts including the glass. Once a year (now or in June, whichever you prefer), clean all parts with a copper sulfate solution, mixed at the rate of one-third pound to 2 gallons of water.

Third Weekend of January. Feed growing plants with a half-strength solution of fertilizer. Maintain your vigilant watch for signs of pests. Begin the forcing process for pots of well-rooted hardy bulbs brought in from a cold place. Sow any of the seeds listed at the end of this chapter. Clean your tools. Give the handles a coating of bright-colored enamel. Write out labels for seeds and bulbs as they arrive. Attach the labels to packets or paper bag with masking tape. This pleasant January activity saves hours of precious time later in the year.

Fourth Weekend of January. Your best efforts to start the year with a clean greenhouse will need fortification now. Bring in a few more pots of bulbs for forcing. If you have the space to experiment, plant six gladiolus corms in a 12-inch pot or tub. These will give extra early bloom in the greenhouse, or you can use them to decorate your patio for the first brunch of the outdoor-living season.

In my experience, tomatoes need ten weeks' growth before being planted outside. If your average date of last killing frost is April 15th, you will need to plant tomato seeds in late January or the first of February. To start tomato seeds, I fill twelve 2¼-inch pots with a mixture of equal parts garden loam, peat moss, and sand, then plant a few hybrid seeds in each. Later these are thinned to leave one seedling in each pot. In February, I start six 2¼-inch pots each of hot and sweet peppers, and in March six 3-inch pots of cucumbers the same way. All this saves transplanting time, and gets the plants off to a rapid start with minimum trouble on my part.

FLOWERING PLANTS FOR JANUARY

Abutilon	Cineraria	Gerbera
Acalypha	Citrus	Gloxinia
African Violet	Clematis	Gypsophila
Amaryllis	Coleus	Heliotrope
Ardisia	Columnea	Hibiscus, Chinese
Aster, China	Crocus	Hyacinth
Azalea	Crossandra	Impatiens
Begonia	Cyclamen	Iris, Dutch
Beloperone	Cyrtanthus	Ixora
Bougainvillea	Daffodil	Jacobinia
Bouvardia	Didiscus	Jasminum
Browallia	Echeveria	Kalanchoe
Cacti	Episcia	Lachenalia
Capsicum	Euphorbia	Lantana
Calendula	Exacum	Lapeirousia
Calla-Lily	Felicia	Marigold
Camellia	Freesia	Mignonette
Centaurea	Gardenia	Myosotis
Cestrum	Gazania	Narcissus
Chrysanthemum	Geranium	Nasturtium

FLOWERING PLANTS FOR JANUARY
[*Continued*]

Nicotiana
Orchid: Cattleya
Orchid: Oncidium
  Splendidum
Orchid: Oncidium
  Tigrinum
Osmanthus
Oxalis

Pansy
Pentas
Petunia
Poinsettia
Primula
Rose
Salvia
Smithiantha

Snapdragon
Solanum
Stevia
Stock
Tulbaghia
Tulip
Ursinia

DIVIDING AND REPOTTING TO DO IN JANUARY

African Violet
Begonia

Clerodendrum
Geranium

Orchids

CUTTINGS TO MAKE IN JANUARY

Ageratum
Beloperone
Browallia
Campanula

Carnation
Clerodendrum
Crassula

Crossandra
Gardenia
Geranium

BULBS TO PLANT IN JANUARY

Amaryllis
Calla-Lily (yellow or pink)
Gloxinia

SEEDS TO PLANT IN JANUARY

African Violet
Azalea
Begonia
Browallia
Calendula
Candytuft
Celosia
Centaurea
Clarkia
Didiscus

Felicia
Gerbera
Gloxinia
Godetia
Gypsophila
Impatiens
Kalanchoe
Lobelia
Marigold
Nierembergia

Petunia (Double
  Grandifloras)
Salpiglossis
Schizanthus
Snapdragon
Solanum
Sweet Alyssum
Sweet Pea
Ursinia

2. February

Outdoors the sky is winter gray, but in the greenhouse there is the blue of summer. Ageratum, browallia, exacum, felicia, myosotis, and clematis bloom like swatches of a heavenly June day. There is the freshness of spring as Dutch irises, tulips, and daffodils unfold dewy petals, and marguerites reflect the sunny mood of a meadow in May. Purple-flowered heliotrope, trained to tree form, opens rich clusters of fragrant bloom, with pink king's crown *(Jacobinia carnea)* in a royal display beneath. In the southeast corner of my greenhouse in February there are the warm colors of the annual flowers of July—beloperone, bougainvillea 'California Gold,' and Chinese hibiscus—and across the aisle, in what I've come to know is a cool microclimate, are nearly bursting buds of calceolarias and cinerarias.

Lengthening days cast a feeling of optimism over the greenhouse this month, and the propagation of plants goes into full swing. You can be freer with the fertilizer—I go to biweekly feedings at container-recommended strength unless the month proves uncommonly cloudy and damp. In February, and again before frost in fall, I am thankful that most of the area underneath my benches is not regularly occupied. By the end of this month, seedlings, pots of spring bulbs, and maturing cinerarias, calceolarias, and other spring flowers will crowd every semidormant plant from the benches and shelves to the floor.

HOW TO START SEEDS

Seed starting on a well-timed schedule is the key to a flowering greenhouse. After you have purchased quality seeds, your next step is selection of a growing medium. I have tried peat moss and sand, peat moss and vermiculite, peat moss

13   This lean-to greenhouse with garlands of English ivy trailing from the benches is open to a living room so that its beauty is always on view. LORD & BURNHAM

and perlite, milled sphagnum moss, and screened, pasteurized potting soil; but horticultural vermiculite is my favorite. It is lightweight (with one hand I can carry a bag half as big as I am), sterile, inexpensive, and available locally. I fill 4- x 6-inch fiberboard flats or bulb pans with vermiculite to within a half-inch of the top. Seeds are then broadcast evenly over the surface. If dust-fine, they are not covered. Larger seeds are covered with vermiculite to a depth of approximately their own thickness.

After I finish the day's seed sowing, I turn the hose to a generous trickle and moisten every flat and bulb pan. These are grouped in sunny parts of the greenhouse, or under fluorescent lights in the basement (see Chapter 1). I watch daily, and add water if necessary to keep the vermiculite evenly moist. With this method I do not cover the starting containers with glass or plastic. As a result, seedlings are accustomed to open air from the beginning. At 55 to 75 degrees, the temperature range of my greenhouse from January until late May, and with the humidifier set at 75 per cent, all seeds germinate readily, even difficult kinds like delphinium, reputed to require a period at 40 degrees to break dormancy. When seedlings have been up seven to ten days I begin weekly feedings of half-strength Ra-Pid-Gro (23-21-17).

With this care, seedlings soon crowd for space and require transplanting, either to individual 2¼-inch pots, or to 2 x 2 spacing in flats. I give first consideration to kinds started for the greenhouse. If I run out of space, I can always pick up bedding plants like ageratum, petunia, and snapdragon at the local garden center. Whether or not I have space, I find inevitably that I accumulate at least fifty packets of seeds for the outdoor garden. I plant most of these in March so that they can be transplanted directly to well-prepared soil in the garden around the middle of May.

I use vermiculite also for cuttings. When new roots are evident, I begin feeding biweekly with Ra-Pid-Gro. Plants take in this fertilizer through foliage as well as roots. I splash it on generously. The leaves take on a healthy luster, and soon the new plants can go into pots of soil.

After transplanting seedlings and cuttings, I clean out the starting containers and add the used vermiculite to my compost pile.

First Weekend of February. Put feeding at the top of your list, but as you make the rounds, look for pests and diseases. There are many seeds to sow now for greenhouse flowers. For example, schizanthus (poor man's orchid) planted now will give May flowers. Transplant to 3-inch pots;

pinch back to induce branching. Shift on to 5's before bloom time.

If you want an abundance of early-flowering annuals for your outdoor garden in summer, February is the ideal time for sowing most kinds. To start non-transplantables like bush sweet peas, sow individual seeds in 2¼-inch pots of vermiculite. Keep warm and moist. Feed biweekly after growth is apparent, and keep in a sunny, airy atmosphere. By the time you have planting-out weather, these will be near the budding stage. Here are some seeds you can sow this weekend for your outdoor garden.

Ageratum
Arctotis
Aster, China
Browallia
Calendula
Candytuft
Carnation, Hardy
Celosia
Centaurea cyanus
Cineraria maritima 'Diamond'
Coleus
Cosmos
Dahlia Coltness and Unwins
Dianthus chinensis heddewiggi
Gazania
Grevillea
Hibiscus Golden Bowl
Lobelia
Marigold
Nemesia
Nicotiana
Nierembergia
Pansy
Perilla
Periwinkle
Petunia
Phlox drummondi
Salpiglossis
Salvia
Scabiosa
Snapdragon
Stock
Sweet Alyssum
Sweet Pea
Torenia
Verbena
Vinca rosea
Zinnia

Second Weekend of February. Vegetative propagation by cuttings and divisions can go into full swing now. This is the time when I make quantities of coleus and dusty miller (*Cineraria maritima* 'Diamond') cuttings in order to carry out a yearly planting outdoors that combines foliage colors of golden chartreuse, mahogany, and silver. Check the lists at the end of this chapter for repotting you may need to do now, and for bulbs to plant. Tuberous begonias started in February will give flowers for Mother's Day, well ahead of summer heat in most areas.

Third Weekend of February. After feeding and pest control, sow some more seeds. Whenever you have a considerable quantity to plant, space sowings two weeks apart so that all seedlings will not need to be transplanted at the same time.

Fourth Weekend of February. Cleanup and catch-up now. There will hardly be any time in March to do what should have been done in February. Groom mature plants. Transplant seedlings and rooted cuttings. Bring in the last pots of bulbs for forcing. Check your supplies. You may need to stop at the garden center for pots, labels, stakes, plant ties, fertilizer, pesticides, or soil mixture ingredients.

FLOWERING PLANTS FOR FEBRUARY

Abutilon	Didiscus	Myosotis
Acacia	Echeveria	Narcissus
Acalypha	Episcia	Nasturtium
African Violet	Euphorbia	Nemesia
Ageratum	Exacum	Nicotiana
Amaryllis	Felicia	Orchid: Epidendrum
Anemone	Freesia	fragrans
Ardisia	Gardenia	Orchid: Oncidium
Aster, China	Gazania	splendidum
Azalea	Geranium	Orchid: Phalaenopsis
Begonia	Gerbera	'Texas Pink'
Bellis	Gladiolus	Osmanthus
Beloperone	Gloxinia	Oxalis
Bougainvillea	Gypsophila	Pansy
Bouvardia	Heliotrope	Pentas
Browallia	Hibiscus, Chinese	Petunia
Cacti	Hyacinth	Poinsettia
Calendula	Impatiens	Primula
Calceolaria	Iris, Dutch	Rose
Calla-Lily	Ixia	Salvia
Camellia	Ixora	Schizanthus
Capsicum	Jacobinia	Smithiantha
Centaurea	Jasminum	Snapdragon
Cestrum	Kalanchoe	Solanum
Cineraria	Lachenalia	Stevia
Citrus	Lantana	Stock
Clematis	Lapeirousia	Sweet Pea
Coleus	Larkspur	Tulbaghia
Crocus	Marguerite	Tulip
Crossandra	Marigold	Ursinia
Cyclamen	Mignonette	Veltheimia

REPOTTING AND DIVIDING TO DO IN FEBRUARY

Abutilon	Kaempferia
African Violet	Orchids
Agapanthus	Strelitzia
Begonia	Tulbaghia

CUTTINGS TO MAKE IN FEBRUARY

Acalypha
Ageratum
Allamanda
Beloperone
Campanula
Cestrum

Clerodendrum
Coleus
Crassula
Crossandra
Croton

Dipladenia
Dusty Miller
Gardenia
Lantana
Tibouchina

BULBS TO PLANT IN FEBRUARY

Achimenes
Agapanthus
Amaryllis

Begonia, Tuberous
Caladium
Calla-Lily (yellow and pink)
Gloxinia

SEEDS TO PLANT IN FEBRUARY

African Violet
Ageratum
Azalea
Begonia
Cacti
Celosia
Coleus
Felicia

Freesia
Gerbera
Gloriosa
Gloxinia
Gypsophila
Kalanchoe
Lobelia
Nierembergia

Petunia
Schizanthus
Snapdragon
Solanum
Spathiphyllum
Stevia
Verbena

3. March

Dreams of a greenhouse filled with flowers come true this month. There are bouquets of cinerarias, every plant covered with daisies of unmatched brilliance. Calceolarias open pocketbook flowers in fiesta colors, and, picking up the theme, *Oncidium splendidum* wafts dancing-girl orchids into the air. Pansies, oxalis, bougainvillea, calendulas, geraniums, impatiens, lantanas, nasturtiums, and Thumbelina zinnias carry on the riot of color. But there is dignity too in this dazzling flower show: a Dutch hybrid amaryllis with flowers of pristine white, fairy primroses blooming in delicate heather colors, the last fragrant freesias of the season, and baskets of sweet alyssum like a fall of snow.

March is a month of great activity in the home greenhouse. Keep a firm hand on the schedule you developed when there was less to do. Work can easily pile up now, and then the gardener is tempted to go grasshoppery from one thing to another. This experience led me to the work plan that I have carried into this book—lists of things to do by weekends. Sometimes I put in an hour or two early in the morning, or at night, so that the work of one weekend doesn't encroach on that of the next.

This is a month of abundant bloom. And it follows that your program of good housekeeping will intensify. Keep fading blooms off plants and in your wastebasket. Tend pest control carefully. Watering is required more frequently. Be sure automatic ventilators and the exhaust fan are working properly. At no time in the year is my greenhouse more flower-filled and fragrant than in March.

First Weekend of March. While you go about the feeding routine, look for aphids, mealybugs, red-spider mites, scale, or other pests. A minor infestation this weekend could be major by next. At the end of this chapter you will find a list of seeds to sow now for flowers for your greenhouse; this is also the time to start seeds for the outdoor garden.

14 *This redwood and glass, free-standing home greenhouse has lath shading on the south-facing roofspan and wall. Circulating fans and a water-misting system cool and humidify the air. A giant staghorn fern,* Platycerium grande, *grows near the roof peak.* HAROLD DAVIS

A list of annual flowers and vegetables that benefit from
an early start indoors is included in Chapter 2.

Second Weekend of March. This is the time to channel all
efforts to the greenhouse. Repot and divide. Put in cuttings
to assure a future of vigorous, young plants for the greenhouse. Plant bulbs of achimenes, tuberous begonias, caladiums, calla-lilies (yellow and pink), and haemanthus. This
may not sound like a busy weekend, but repotting and
dividing even two or three plants has a way of leading
from one thing to another, like pulling crabgrass in July.
Before all this pleasant activity becomes work, take a break.
Sit down for a cup of tea and feast your eyes on the flower
show.

Third Weekend of March. This is a repeat of the first
one. Apply a full round of liquid fertilizer. Take care of
pest control. Plant seeds for greenhouse flowers (see list
at end of chapter).

Fourth Weekend of March. By now you have a healthy
cache of seedlings started for the summer garden, and for
your greenhouse. Be sure they have ample light, fresh air,
moisture, and fertilizer. If you have a perennial border, this
is a good time to sow seeds of some new kinds, or to re-
plenish those you have already. Transplant later to nursery
rows in your outside work center, or to an out of the way,
protected part of the garden. This place needs to be easily
reached with the hose for frequent watering in dry periods,
and convenient to your comings and goings. Seedlings started
now will be vigorous clumps by September, ready for permanent planting in the border.

FLOWERING PLANTS FOR MARCH

Abutilon	Bellis	Citrus
Acacia	Beloperone	Clarkia
Acalypha	Bougainvillea	Clematis
African Violet	Browallia	Clerodendrum
Agapanthus	Cacti	Clivia
Ageratum	Calceolaria	Coleus
Amaryllis	Calendula	Columnea
Anemone	Calla-Lily	Crocus
Anthurium	Camellia	Crossandra
Ardisia	Capsicum	Cyclamen
Aster, China	Centaurea	Didiscus
Azalea	Cestrum	Dimorphotheca
Begonia	Cineraria	Echeveria

FLOWERING PLANTS FOR MARCH
[*Continued*]

Episcia
Euphorbia
Exacum
Felicia
Freesia
Gardenia
Gazania
Geranium
Gerbera
Gladiolus
Gloriosa
Gloxinia
Gypsophila
Heliotrope
Hibiscus, Chinese
Hoya
Hyacinth
Hydrangea
Impatiens
Iris, Dutch
Ixia
Ixora
Jacobinia
Kalanchoe

Lachenalia
Lantana
Lapeirousia
Larkspur
Lily
Marguerite
Marigold
Mignonette
Myosotis
Narcissus
Nasturtium
Nemesia
Nicotiana
Nierembergia
Orchid: Cattleya
   'Ave Maria'
Orchid: Epidendrum
   Fragrans
Orchid: Oncidium
   Ampliatum Majus
Orchid: Oncidium
   Splendidum
Ornithogalum
Osmanthus

Oxalis
Pansy
Passiflora
Pentas
Petunia
Primula
Ranunculus
Rose
Salvia
Schizanthus
Snapdragon
Spathiphyllum
Stephanotis
Stock
Strelitzia
Sweet Alyssum
Sweet Pea
Tibouchina
Tulbaghia
Tulip
Ursinia
Veltheimia
Zinnia

REPOTTING AND DIVIDING TO DO IN MARCH

Abutilon
African Violet
Agapanthus
Allamanda
Ardisia

Begonia
Beloperone
Cacti
Camellia
Capsicum

Croton
Haemanthus
Kaempferia
Orchids
Strelitzia

SEEDS TO PLANT IN MARCH

Abutilon
Acacia
African Violet
Anthurium
Ardisia
Azalea
Begonia
Browallia

Cacti
Camellia
Celosia
Clivia
Felicia
Freesia
Gloriosa
Gypsophila

Kalanchoe
Nerium
Primula
Smithiantha
Solanum
Spathiphyllum

CUTTINGS TO MAKE IN MARCH

Acalypha
Allamanda
Aphelandra
Ardisia
Beloperone
Bouvardia
Cacti
Cestrum
Clerodendrum
Coleus
Columnea

Crassula
Crossandra
Croton
Dipladenia
Echeveria
Episcia
Euphorbia
Gardenia
Geranium
Hibiscus, Chinese
Hoya

Ixora
Jasminum
Lantana
Nerium
Passiflora
Salvia
Stephanotis
Stevia
Tibouchina

BULBS TO PLANT IN MARCH

Achimenes
Begonia, Tuberous

Caladium
Calla-Lily (yellow and pink)
Haemanthus

4. *April*

Floral abundance this month suggests attractive groupings of plants so that each one is fully complemented by its companions. The Easter lily you have forced into bloom will look heavenly with pots of blue lobelia below, a heliotrope standard above and to the back of the bench, and plants of the bright rose-pink geranium 'Genie' all around. Make a plain green setting of foliage plants for *Paphiopedilum maudiae* in its moment of glory. Elsewhere mass flowering plants into a breathtaking display—acacia, acalypha, begonia, cineraria, clarkia, fuchsia, gerbera, godetia, nemesia, and salvia. When all is in place, invite your friends to an "Open Greenhouse" and hope that the passion vine unfolds a flower of mystic beauty for the occasion.

April in the home greenhouse is like March—only more so. Lack of space becomes acute, and before weekend activities proceed, it may be necessary to alleviate this problem. As soon as forced bulbs finish blooming, transfer them to a coldframe outdoors. In the absence of spring rains, they will need to be watered. It is a good idea to protect the greenhouse-pampered foliage from severe freezing by lowering the sash on cold nights.

I solve space problems in several ways. My collection of nearly seventy hybrid amaryllis goes under the benches from now until they are placed outdoors in late May or early June. Pots of chrysanthemums that bloomed during the winter, and spent recent weeks under the benches, are moved to the coldframe. Finally, in near desperation I usually have to part with some large specimen plants that have lost the vigor of youth. One year I added fluorescent lights in a growing area of my basement, but that is filled with plants now. Another season I added glass shelves along the sides of my greenhouse, but they too are filled to capacity. Of course, these offer prime space for starting seeds, so no matter what holds forth on them, it gets lowered to the bench, or below, in favor of the new generation.

April is an unpredictable month all over the country. It can be cold and rainy, or dry, windy, and sunny. In any event, with seedlings coming along, it is a month to ventilate freely, and to water attentively. Shading may be necessary, depending of course on the efficiency of your ventilating system, and on the kind of plants you grow. My shade-loving types are grouped on a part of the benches shaded at this time of the year by a French hybrid grapevine, and also to some extent by espaliered rose geraniums that extend now to over a third of the south side of my greenhouse. If you favor more traditional means of shading, see Chapter 5.

PLAN A GARDEN WORK CENTER AROUND
YOUR GREENHOUSE

It is at this time of year when a work center becomes a valuable adjunct to home greenhouse gardening. This is the place for a coldframe, an outdoor potting bench to use in pleasant weather, shelves to display container plants, and a lath house. Even though you have a good potting place inside your greenhouse, a lot of messy work can be done outdoors thus avoiding major cleanup in the greenhouse. Ideally, this area also provides storage for garden loam, peat moss, and sand, a large container of vermiculite or sphagnum moss, the lawn mower, and miscellaneous hand tools like rakes, shovels, and trowels.

A lath house can be a decided convenience in the work center. Its primary function is to protect greenhouse plants while they are outdoors in summer. Yours may be a jungle-like place with an abundance of hanging baskets, and vines clambering all around. Or you may favor plenty of clean, open space for your outdoor furniture with plants grouped neatly against the walls. The most recent American use of lath shelters has been for summer display of bonsai collections. However you plan to use a lath house, keep these construction guidelines in mind: Use weather-resistant material like redwood with 4 x 4 uprights set in concrete footings, 2 x 4 rafters, and 1 x 2's instead of regular lath.

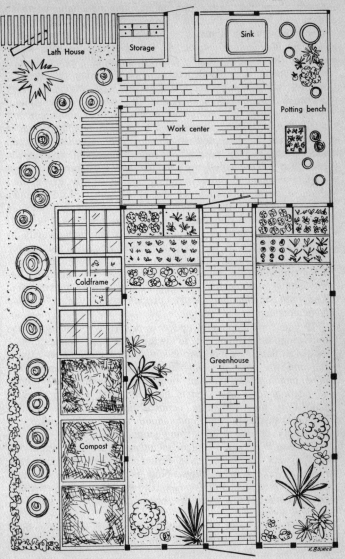

Lath House

Storage

Sink

Work center

Potting bench

Coldframe

Greenhouse

Compost

K. BOURKE

FIGURE 3 *Garden work center planned around a home greenhouse.*

Space about one lath width apart, and run laths north to south so that as the sun moves, the shade also moves slowly across the plants.

First Weekend of April. As in other months, this weekend is the time to feed, seed, and control pests. I start off a typical first April weekend on Saturday morning by mixing liquid houseplant fertilizer and applying it to every plant in the greenhouse. Along the way I make mental notes of plants that need special attention or some control.

Seedlings started earlier need transplanting. There was a time when I attempted to move every seedling into an individual 2¼-inch peat pot. While this worked well for the plants, it nearly killed me. As long as I attempted such a feat, I never had time to enjoy spring in my greenhouse or as it came outdoors with the early bulbs. More recently I have expedited the procedure. I sow in flats and pots of pure vermiculite. Seedlings are fed biweekly with 23-21-17. As soon as danger of frost is past, I transplant directly to blooming places in the garden. Some seedlings are gangly from being crowded, but if I nip out the tips a few days after transplanting, bushiness is soon evident. Seedlings being brought along for my greenhouse receive better care. They are transplanted at the proper time, even if all else is neglected.

If you have time and space to transplant seedlings onto individual containers, or to space them out about 2 x 2 inches in flats, this weekend easily could be filled from sunup to sundown with this activity. Make yourself comfortable at a bench of convenient height, and have mixed plenty of potting soil: equal parts garden loam, peat moss, and sand (you may substitute vermiculite or perlite for sand). Water transplants well and shade them with newspapers for a day or two until wilting stops.

Second Weekend of April. Cuttings rate first attentions now. Check on those made earlier. Pot any that are well-rooted. Make new cuttings. Now is a good time to start camellia, clematis, and fuchsia cuttings. Use a polyethylene cover, with bottom heat of about 72 degrees, to help the process along.

Repot and divide any plants that need it. Continue bulb planting, including achimenes, tuberous begonias, caladiums, and calla-lilies (yellow or pink).

Third Weekend of April. Apply fertilizer. Check for pests and disease. Act accordingly. There are plenty of seeds to

15 *A lath-house potting shed attached to a home greenhouse helps conserve greenhouse space for growing plants and also provides an area to store necessary supplies. During warm weather the greenhouse can be emptied for cleaning and the plants kept inside the lath house.* MAYNARD PARKER

be sown now for blooms next fall, winter, and spring in the greenhouse. If, after you have done these chores, you have any time left, there will be transplanting and clean-up work to do. In most areas, more hours are needed outdoors each weekend.

Fourth Weekend of April. While watering and greenhouse clean-up continue to take more time, the season is advancing so that you will need to spend a lion's share of this weekend (if it is sunny) outdoors. For one thing, seedlings will do better transplanted to open ground if they have had first a week to ten days outdoors in a protected place. A coldframe is ideal for this purpose, especially if frost is predicted. Then all you have to do is lower the sash and cover with blankets until the temperature rises safely. But this is a critical time. Tender seedlings accustomed to the closeness of the greenhouse atmosphere will dry out quickly and sear rapidly. Keep the growing medium evenly moist. Shield from strong wind and hard rain.

FLOWERING PLANTS FOR APRIL

Abutilon
Acacia
Acalypha
African Violet
Agapanthus
Ageratum
Amaryllis
Anemone
Anthurium
Ardisia
Aster, China
Azalea
Begonia
Bellis
Beloperone
Bougainvillea
Browallia
Cacti
Caladium
Calceolaria
Calendula
Calla-Lily
Camellia
Candytuft
Centaurea
Cestrum
Cineraria
Citrus
Clarkia
Clematis
Clerodendrum

Clivia
Coleus
Columnea
Crossandra
Cyclamen
Didiscus
Dimorphotheca
Echeveria
Episcia
Euphorbia
Exacum
Felicia
Fuchsia
Gardenia
Gazania
Geranium
Gerbera
Gladiolus
Gloriosa
Gloxinia
Godetia
Gypsophila
Heliotrope
Hibiscus, Chinese
Hoya
Impatiens
Iris, Dutch
Ixia
Ixora
Jacobinia
Kaempferia

Kalanchoe
Lachenalia
Lantana
Larkspur
Lily
Lobelia
Marguerite
Marigold
Mignonette
Myosotis
Nasturtium
Nemesia
Nicotiana
Nierembergia
Orchid: Cattleya
  skinneri
Orchid: Epidendrum
  fragrans
Orchid: Oncidium
  ampliatum majus
Orchid: Paphiopedi-
  lum Maudiae
Osmanthus
Oxalis
Pansy
Passiflora
Pentas
Petunia
Primula
Ranunculus
Rose

FLOWERING PLANTS FOR APRIL
[*Continued*]

Salpiglossis
Salvia
Schizanthus
Snapdragon
Spathiphyllum
Stephanotis

Stock
Strelitzia
Sweet Alyssum
Sweet Pea
Tibouchina
Tulbaghia

Tulip
Ursinia
Veltheimia
Zinnia

REPOTTING AND DIVIDING TO DO IN APRIL

Abutilon
African Violet
Ardisia

Begonia
Cacti
Camellia

Haemanthus
Orchids
Strelitzia

CUTTINGS TO MAKE IN APRIL

Acalypha
Allamanda
Aphelandra
Ardisia
Beloperone
Bougainvillea
Bouvardia
Cacti
Cestrum
Chrysanthemum
Columnea

Crassula
Crossandra
Croton
Dipladenia
Echeveria
Euphorbia
Gardenia
Geranium
Hibiscus, Chinese
Hoya
Hydrangea

Ixora
Jasminum
Lantana
Marguerite
Nerium
Passiflora
Pentas
Salvia
Stephanotis
Stevia
Tibouchina

BULBS TO PLANT IN APRIL

Achimenes
Begonia, Tuberous

Caladium
Calla-Lily (yellow or pink)
Gladiolus

SEEDS TO PLANT IN APRIL

Abutilon
Acacia
African Violet
Anemone
Anthurium
Ardisia
Aster, China

Begonia
Browallia
Cacti
Capsicum
Celosia
Cineraria
Clivia

Felicia
Gypsophila
Kalanchoe
Nerium
Primula
Smithiantha
Solanum

5. May

Seedlings and cuttings started early for the garden, and transplanted to individual 2¼'s or 3's, bloom now with all the promise of summer. There are 'Petite' marigolds, petunias, dwarf zinnias, ageratums, wax begonias, impatiens, and lantanas. Gloxinias started in January open velvety trumpets, and the beauty of a blue hydrangea brings with it a feeling of special accomplishment for the gardener. Then comes the climax of spring: a cattleya orchid unfurls the first of many treasured flowers.

Whether or not you shade your greenhouse will depend on how you use it in summer and what you grow inside. At one time I shaded my greenhouse heavily from about March 1 until October 15th. Then one year I did not get the shading material on until much later—early June, in fact—and I was amazed at how much better my plants fared through the spring months. Geraniums bloomed as never before, and seedlings were the stockiest I had ever grown.

GREENHOUSE SHADING AND COOLING

The ideal air-conditioning for a home greenhouse in warm weather is an evaporative cooler to lower temperatures and raise humidity, combined with not-too-dense shading material. The result will be moist, cool air, and enough foot-candles of light to keep plants reasonably compact and in bloom.

Lumite saran shade cloth is a greenhouse shading material recently made available to home gardeners. It is a dark green plastic fabric made in a variety of weaves that gives various sun-shade combinations. The cloth gives uniform shade—no hot spots, no dull areas. It is wind-resistant; will not rust, rot, or mildew. Lumite saran cloth can be sewn to fit like an electric toaster cover over a greenhouse

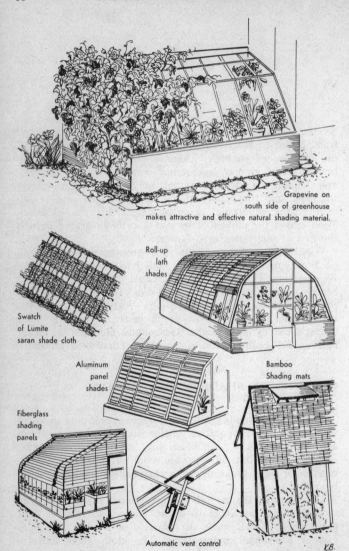

Grapevine on south side of greenhouse makes attractive and effective natural shading material.

Swatch of Lumite saran shade cloth

Roll-up lath shades

Aluminum panel shades

Bamboo Shading mats

Fiberglass shading panels

Automatic vent control

K.B.

FIGURE 4   *Ideas for shading and cooling a home greenhouse.*

glazed with glass or any kind of plastic, including polyethylene.

Roll-up lath shades of wood are an excellent and attractive means of shading a greenhouse. They can be adjusted to fit any whim of the weather. These are usually coated with aluminum paint to preserve the wood and reflect heat, and come in factory-assembled rolls to fit the greenhouse.

Everyone who shades a greenhouse wants something atatractive, effective, maintenance-free, and inexpensive. Aluminum panel shades rate high by such a check list. They are made of aluminum slats fastened to wooden frames painted with aluminum. Naturally, these must be attached to the greenhouse, and it is no small matter to remove them during a period of cloudy weather.

Corrugated fiberglass shading panels, usually in a pastel shade of green, are an excellent choice. These are lightweight, easily installed, and they reduce light by 31 per cent. This light reduction is a diffusion that blends sun and shade into a desirable intensity for most plants.

Various kinds of whitewash and bamboo screens are the least expensive means of shading. Some manufacturers of pre-fabricated greenhouses have a long-lasting paste that is thinned with benzine or gasoline. It gives good shading, and is available in white or light green, but it looks awful to you and the neighbors. All paintlike shading materials are placed on the glass in late winter or early spring. By autumn most of the shading will have washed or flaked off.

Rolls of bamboo, either matchstick or half-inch size, make effective, good-looking shades, but the cord that binds the bamboo together tends to rot within a few years, particularly in moist climates. But bamboo shading costs less and is available at most local department or hardware stores, not to mention mail-order firms such as Sears and Wards.

Cooling a greenhouse by evaporation is an effective means of making a greenhouse more practicable in summer. Here is how the system works: The hot outdoor air is pulled by a fan through wet aspen pads to make a relatively cool and moist atmosphere inside. The drier your climate, of course, the better an evaporative cooler can function. To figure the size cooler you need, select one with an air capacity 50 per cent greater than the cubic volume of your greenhouse. To arrive at this figure, multiply length x width x average height.

Depending on local humidity conditions, an evaporative cooler combined effectively with a shading material can lower temperature by as much as 30 degrees from that outdoors. Evaporative coolers can be thermostatically controlled so that they will labor only during the daytime.

Under Glass readers who answered my questionnaire provided a wealth of good ideas for improving summer conditions in a home greenhouse. Removal of side Mylar plastic panels and replacing them with panels of screen was one popular means of cooling, especially in the South. Lumite saran shading cloth of 50 per cent density was also a frequent choice. One grower in Texas recommends redwood slats on top for shade and as a means of hail protection, with Venetian blinds inside on each 2-foot side section for increased light control. From Dallas came a report of the use of redwood slats on the roof all year, but nothing on the sides, so that when inside the greenhouse a person has the feeling of being outdoors. This 14 x 21 foot house is cooled by an evaporative cooler, and a bougainvillea shades the west end in summer.

A San Antonio grower with a 14 x 18 foot house for African violets, gloxinias, and other gesneriads reports use of 80 per cent Lumite saran shading cloth in summer, with evaporative cooling. Cheesecloth is used in winter in place of the saran. Another Dallas correspondent with a 15 x 30 house reported no shade from November to April, but full shade the balance of the year, combined with a large evaporative cooler.

From Rhode Island came a four-point program for summer climate control in a 12 x 15 foot greenhouse: (1) shades, (2) automatic vents, (3) fine spray of water on walks when very hot, and (4) large maple tree nearby for natural shading and cooling.

A man in Illinois uses a large roll of peeled bamboo over the greenhouse top. This is lowered around hail time in May, and left until November. It is held about 1½ inches above the glass by means of wooden strips. In addition, this house is cooled by a roof vent, a screen in the door, a small suction fan in the roof, and a humidifier.

First Weekend of May. Most greenhouses are veritable flower shows now. Routine maintenance is all the more important. Feed every ten days to two weeks. Keep pests under control. Be sure the soil is evenly moist all the time. Start the month with your feeding rounds, and jot down

notes of pest control that will be needed before you go
back to work on Monday.

The transplanting of crowded seedlings may well take
the rest of your time. The outdoor garden is likely to need
attention, too. Except in the deep South, there is still
time to start a few seeds of cucumbers, melons, and squash
in 3-inch peat pots of rich, humusy soil. These will be ready
to transplant outdoors, pot and all, about June 1, or when
the weather is settled and warm. If you can still find a
place to sow, check this month's listing of seeds to plant
for future greenhouse blooms. There are all kinds of pos-
sibilities.

Second Weekend of May. Transplanting of seedlings may
well go on in every spare minute this weekend, but it is
also a good time to repot and divide most of the permanent
greenhouse plants. The list at the end of this chapter suggests a few, but actually, this is such good growing time
that almost all transplanting can proceed with reasonable
assurance of success. Take cuttings. Practically all perennial greenhouse plants will root readily now. Before hot
weather, sow perennial seeds for the outdoor garden.

Third Weekend of May. Put feeding and pest control at
the top of your list. And it is a good time for general
clean-up. In your remaining time (what time?), transplant
seedlings and look ahead to next weekend. Begin to get
ready for the big move.

Fourth Weekend of May. Make this target date for the
final moving-out of all plants that are to spend the summer outdoors. Keep them as much together as possible;
you will be glad of this when daily watering becomes a
necessity. A few clusters of lonely plants scattered over
the yard are sure to be neglected. I have one group on
north-facing shelves along the 6-foot redwood fence in
front of the greenhouse. These are on view from the outdoor living area, so I change the display occasionally to
keep it interesting. All my other plants are grouped along
the north side of the redwood fence that borders our lot.

FLOWERING PLANTS FOR MAY

Abutilon	Amaryllis	Begonia
African Violet	Anthurium	Bellis
Agapanthus	Ardisia	Beloperone
Ageratum	Aster, China	Browallia

FLOWERING PLANTS FOR MAY
[*Continued*]

Cacti
Caladium
Calceolaria
Calendula
Calla-Lily
Candytuft
Capsicum
Celosia
Centaurea
Cestrum
Cineraria
Citrus
Clarkia
Clematis
Clerodendrum
Clivia
Coleus
Columnea
Crassula
Crossandra
Didiscus
Dimorphotheca
Episcia
Euphorbia
Exacum
Felicia
Fuchsia
Gardenia
Gazania
Geranium

Gerbera
Gloriosa
Gloxinia
Godetia
Gypsophila
Haemanthus
Heliotrope
Hibiscus, Chinese
Hoya
Hydrangea
Impatiens
Ixora
Jacobinia
Jasminum
Kaempferia
Kalanchoe
Lantana
Larkspur
Lobelia
Marguerite
Marigold
Mignonette
Nasturtium
Nemesia
Nerium
Nicotiana
Nierembergia
Orchid: Brassolaelio-
    cattleya 'Ojai'
Orchid: Epidendrum

fragrans
Orchid: Oncidium
    ampliatum majus
Orchid: Paphiopedi-
    lum Maudiae
Osmanthus
Oxalis
Pansy
Passiflora
Pentas
Petunia
Primula
Ranunculus
Rose
Salpiglossis
Salvia
Schizanthus
Snapdragon
Spathiphyllum
Stephanotis
Stock
Strelitzia
Sweet Alyssum
Sweet Pea
Tibouchina
Tulbaghia
Ursinia
Zinnia

CUTTINGS TO MAKE IN MAY

Acalypha
Aphelandra
Ardisia
Beloperone
Bougainvillea
Bouvardia
Cacti
Cestrum
Chrysanthemum
Citrus

Crassula
Crossandra
Croton
Echeveria
Euphorbia
Felicia
Geranium
Hibiscus, Chinese
Hoya
Ixora

Marguerite
Nerium
Osmanthus
Passiflora
Poinsettia
Salvia
Stephanotis
Stevia
Tibouchina

REPOTTING AND DIVIDING TO DO IN MAY

Abutilon   Cacti
African Violet   Camellia
Ardisia   Haemanthus
Begonia   Orchids

SEEDS TO PLANT IN MAY

Abutilon   Cineraria   Impatiens
African Violet   Clivia   Kalanchoe
Anemone   Coleus   Myosotis
Ardisia   Exacum   Nerium
Begonia   Felicia   Pansy
Browallia   Gazania   Primula
Cacti   Gypsophila   Salvia
Camellia   Heliotrope   Smithiantha

6. June

The atmosphere of the greenhouse changes this month and the stage is set with tropicals. In shade, warmth, and high humidity, such flamboyant beauties as allamanda, *Clerodendrum pleniflorum fragrans*, dipladenia, Chinese hibiscus, anthurium, and strelitzia open exotic blooms. Between these exciting moments the summer show keeps a colorful pace with caladiums, achimenes, episcias, a bench of gloxinia hybrids, kaempferias, smithianthas, and spathiphyllums.

Keep up with your schedule now, and by the end of the month, you will have your greenhouse well on its way to a flowering fall and winter. As the strong sun and heat of summer come on, your keys to a greenhouse atmosphere that is conducive to good growth and inviting to you, lie in good shading, ventilating, watering, and humidifying (Chapter 5).

First Weekend of June. Start with feeding and pest control. If you live far enough north for there to be a few more weeks of cool nights, sow perennial seeds for your garden. If you have not done it already, dry off white calla-lilies, lapeirousias, cyclamen, and lachenalias for a summer rest.

Second Weekend of June. Repot and divide, but only if you must. I recommend instead a complete clean-up of the greenhouse. Take movable plants outdoors to the lath house, or elsewhere near the greenhouse with protection from hot midday sun and hard winds. If you have a choice, the ideal day for this project is a cool, cloudy one. Some gardeners put off the annual clean-up until August, and this is all right, but I prefer June, and early, while I am still fired up from the fast pace of spring gardening. The idea is not to slow down until the greenhouse is in order.

Pull out weeds, trash, and dead plants that have accumulated. Scrub pots and seed flats with a stiff brush and warm, sudsy water. Use steel wool or soap pads if necessary. Rinse in clear water, arrange according to size, and store away in a convenient, out-of-sight place. With benches cleared, give them a scrubbing too. Portable benches that can be taken outdoors for cleaning are a convenience, and while they are out, you can get to the greenhouse walls for a really thorough clean-up.

If yours is a gravel floor, renew it by removing the top inch or two of stones and replacing with fresh ones. Dried petals and algae on greenhouse glass may have to be removed with a razor blade. Wash inside and out. Dirty panes can cut winter sunlight by 30 per cent. If your greenhouse has a brick, stone, or concrete wall, scrub down with a stiff brush, rinse with clear water, then whitewash the inside.

Before you bring back plants, be sure every container is clean. It is important that the plants be free of insect infestations. Many growers take advantage of a cleaned-out greenhouse to fumigate. If you are a fumigator, I am sure you will too. There are too many small children and pets around our yard to risk this method of pest control. I rely instead on preventive maintenance, occasional spot-spraying with a battery-powered unit, and dipping plants to stop a major infestation. The annual complete clean-up of the greenhouse is a further hedge against trouble.

Third Weekend of June. First, take care of feeding, then, if you are like me, the clean-up detail will still have loose ends to be tied up. Pot washing, for example, has a way of getting out of hand. What began as a brisk, direct removal of all litter from the greenhouse, becomes a tedious detail job that may take up every free moment of the weekend. If plants taken from the greenhouse are safely ensconced outdoors, leave them there. With the greenhouse empty, you can accomplish the complete clean-up job.

Sometime this weekend, sow seeds listed at the end of the chapter for future greenhouse bloom. In severely hot climates, you will do better to wait until summer heat breaks in late August or early September, unless, of course, you have an effective cooling system. Transplant seedlings started last month.

Fourth Weekend of June. This is a good time to make cuttings of plants you want to propagate for friends, or to assure your own vigorous crop of future flowers.

At last, a lull in greenhouse chores. If you have kept up with weekend projects since the first of the year, congratulate yourself on being halfway through the year in good shape. It is time to take a rest.

FLOWERING PLANTS FOR JUNE

Abutilon
Achimenes
African Violet
Agapanthus
Allamanda
Anthurium
Aster, China
Begonia
Beloperone
Bougainvillea
Browallia
Cacti
Caladium
Calla-Lily
Campanula
Candytuft
Celosia
Cestrum
Citrus
Clarkia
Clerodendrum
Clivia
Coleus
Columnea
Crassula
Crossandra

Dimorphotheca
Dipladenia
Episcia
Euphorbia
Fuchsia
Gazania
Geranium
Gloxinia
Godetia
Gypsophila
Haemanthus
Hibiscus, Chinese
Hoya
Impatiens
Ixora
Jacobinia
Jasminum
Kaempferia
Lantana
Lobelia
Marguerite
Marigold
Nerium
Nicotiana
Orchid: Epidendrum
   Fragrans

Orchid: Laelio-
   cattleya Canhami-
   ana Alba
Orchid: Paphiopedi-
   lum Maudiae
Osmanthus
Oxalis
Pansy
Passiflora
Pentas
Petunia
Punica
Rose
Salvia
Smithiantha
Snapdragon
Spathiphyllum
Stephanotis
Strelitzia
Sweet Alyssum
Sweet Pea
Tibouchina
Tulbaghia
Zinnia

CUTTINGS TO MAKE IN JUNE

Acacia
Acalypha
Azalea
Beloperone
Bougainvillea
Cacti
Cestrum
Chrysanthemum
Citrus

Clematis
Crassula
Crossandra
Croton
Echeveria
Euphorbia
Felicia
Geranium
Hibiscus, Chinese

Hoya
Marguerite
Nerium
Osmanthus
Passiflora
Poinsettia
Punica
Salvia
Tibouchina

SEEDS TO PLANT IN JUNE

African Violet
Anemone
Begonia
Browallia
Cacti
Calceolaria
Cineraria
Coleus
Cyclamen

Didiscus
Exacum
Felicia
Gazania
Gypsophila
Heliotrope
Impatiens
Kalanchoe
Mignonette

Myosotis
Nerium
Nicotiana
Pansy
Petunia
Primula
Salvia
Smithiantha
Ursinia

DIVIDING AND REPOTTING TO DO IN JUNE

Acacia
African Violet

Begonia
Cacti
Orchids

7. July

July may be the least active month in your greenhouse. From this viewpoint, it is a good time to take a vacation. Whether this is a long weekend, a fortnight, or a month, you will need someone to look after the greenhouse. Make a check list of chores—watering, shading, cooling, ventilating, and pest control—and go over this with the plant-sitter point by point well ahead of your departure.

First Weekend of July. Feeding and pest control is just as vital now as in the marvelous growing weather of May. While temperatures may not be so pleasant, if they are reasonably favorable, and container plants have enough moisture, growth will continue. In the pest department, mealybugs multiply prodigiously in warmth and humidity. Add moisture and nighttime coolness, and there may be slugs. Deal with these slimy creatures of the netherworld by putting out a regular slug-and-snail bait. One effective deterrent is metaldehyde.

This is a good time to project your greenhouse into October, the month when most of us take a more intense interest in indoor gardening, and the time when we want more flowers for the greenhouse. If chrysanthemums are coming along on schedule, with sturdy, pest-free growth, turn your attention to other flowers for October.

Second Weekend of July. This is the time for routine repotting and dividing. Cuttings, too, can go in now. Gloxinias, for example, in full bloom, may yield crisp, medium-sized leaves for inserting into moist vermiculite in a cool, shaded, moist part of the greenhouse, or beneath a protective shrub outdoors. Kept moist, roots soon form. Begin to feed biweekly after this, and continue so long as the leaf is firm. When it begins to yellow naturally, withhold feeding and watering. Dry off. Then unpot, inspect the new tuber that has formed, and plant it in a 5-inch container. Keep barely moist until growth starts.

Third Weekend of July. Another time for feeding and pest control. You can sow seeds of all kinds for your greenhouse, provided you have a place with protection from torrid summer conditions. You can even sow seed of cinerarias if you have a cool basement (a range of about 68 to 75 degrees). Start them there under fluorescent lights, then when plants are well established, move them outdoors to a protected coldframe, or to the greenhouse if it is cooled in summer. In similar conditions you can sow seeds of perennials for the garden; these will be ready to transplant outdoors in late August or early September.

Fourth Weekend of July. Fall catalogs from seedsmen and bulb growers are ready now. Be sure you are on all the mailing lists you want to be.

Does any home greenhouse ever have enough cyclamen for fall to spring bloom? This situation is best remedied by sowing a generous quantity of seeds this weekend.

FLOWERING PLANTS FOR JULY

Abutilon	Dipladenia	Orchid: Epidendrum
Achimenes	Episcia	fragrans
African Violet	Euphorbia	Orchid: Epidendrum
Agapanthus	Fuchsia	tampense
Allamanda	Gazania	Orchid: Paphiopedi-
Anthurium	Geranium	lum Maudiae
Aster, Chinese	Gloxinia	Oxalis
Begonia	Gypsophila	Passiflora
Beloperone	Haemanthus	Pentas
Bougainvillea	Hibiscus, Chinese	Petunia
Cacti	Hoya	Punica
Caladium	Impatiens	Rose
Calla-Lily	Ixora	Smithiantha
Campanula	Jacobinia	Spathiphyllum
Cestrum	Jasminum	Strelitzia
Citrus	Kaempferia	Sweet Pea
Clerodendrum	Lantana	Tibouchina
Coleus	Marguerite	Tulbaghia
Crassula	Nerium	Zinnia
Crossandra		

REPOTTING AND DIVIDING TO DO IN JULY

African Violet
Begonia
Orchids

CUTTINGS TO MAKE IN JULY

Acacia	Crossandra	Osmanthus
Acalypha	Euphorbia	Passiflora
Azalea	Fuchsia	Petunia
Beloperone	Geranium	Poinsettia
Citrus	Heliotrope	Punica
Clematis	Hibiscus, Chinese	Salvia
Coleus	Impatiens	
Crassula	Nerium	

SEEDS TO PLANT IN JULY

African Violet	Gypsophila	Primula
Aster, China	Impatiens	Salvia
Calendula	Kalanchoe	Snapdragon
Celosia	Mignonette	Stock
Coleus	Myosotis	Sweet Alyssum
Cyclamen	Nerium	Sweet Pea
Didiscus	Nicotiana	Ursinia
Dimorphotheca	Pansy	
Felicia	Petunia	

8. *August*

Now is the time for greenhouse repairs and renovations. Start with replacement of broken panes or damaged plastic. Repaint wooden framework.

How about the heating system last year—was it satisfactory? If not, and you planned some improvements, take action now. If you do not have a coldframe or hotbed, install a unit now (Chapter 4).

Did you have enough pots and flats last winter? You will not know the full enjoyment of your greenhouse until you have a supply of pots in as many sizes as you need. I prefer white plastic pots because they are attractive, lightweight, and plants in them require less frequent watering. Flats can be as coarse as a sawed-off cherry crate, or as fancy as a molded, pastel-colored, "everlasting" plastic tray.

First Weekend of August. Feeding and pest control come first. Then take care of cleaning and pickup details. Some pot washing is sure to be in order now. Order bulbs, too. Start with kinds to force—tulips, daffodils, hyacinths, and crocuses. Add generous quantities of freesias, lachenalias, veltheimias, white calla-lilies, oxalis, and brodiaeas. Get at least six *Sternbergia lutea,* too, for a pot of crocuslike, golden flowers in September or early October. After blooming, these can go into a frost-free coldframe for the winter. In spring, plant out permanently in a sunny, well-drained perennial border. Order African violets for September delivery.

Second Weekend of August. Cuttings take precedence now (see the list at the end of this chapter). Try rooting some tip cuttings from your potted azaleas. Insert in moist sand and peat moss; provide shade and high humidity. Transplant to 2¼-inch pots of soil the first of November. These small plants will give some Christmas bloom. Put them at the front of the bench in your greenhouse.

Sow seeds of *Bellis perennis,* cheiranthus, pansies, violas, *Dianthus barbatus,* and forget-me-nots to overplant bulb beds outdoors in early October.

Third Weekend of August. Feeding comes first, then pest control. Seed-sowing, too, can be a part of this weekend's activity. Many annual flowers—calendulas, marigolds, nasturtiums, and nemesias, for example—may be started from seeds sown now for winter and spring bloom.

Fourth Weekend of August. Plant several pots of fall- and winter-flowering oxalis. Include *O. braziliensis, O. melanosticta, O. ortgiesi, O. pes-caprae* (formerly *O. cernua*), *O. regnelli,* and *O. rubra* (sometimes called *O. crassipes*).

FLOWERING PLANTS FOR AUGUST

Abutilon
Achimenes
African Violet
Agapanthus
Allamanda
Anthurium
Aster, China
Begonia
Beloperone
Bougainvillea
Cacti
Caladium
Calla-Lily
Campanula
Celosia
Cestrum
Citrus
Clerodendrum
Coleus
Columnea
Crassula

Crossandra
Dipladenia
Episcia
Euphorbia
Fuchsia
Gazania
Geranium
Gloxinia
Gypsophila
Haemanthus
Hibiscus, Chinese
Hoya
Impatiens
Ixora
Jacobinia
Jasminum
Kaempferia
Lantana
Marguerite
Nerium

Orchid: Cattleya
  'Enid H.'
Orchid: Brassavola
  nodosa
Orchid: Epidendrum
  fragrans
Orchid: Paphiopedi-
  lum Maudiae
Oxalis
Passiflora
Pentas
Petunia
Punica
Rose
Smithiantha
Spathiphyllum
Strelitzia
Sweet Pea
Tibouchina
Tulbaghia
Zinnia

REPOTTING AND DIVIDING TO DO IN AUGUST

African Violet
Begonia

Orchid
Veltheimia

CUTTINGS TO MAKE IN AUGUST

Ageratum
Azalea
Beloperone
Camellia
Coleus

Crassula
Crossandra
Fuchsia
Geranium
Impatiens

Nerium
Passiflora
Petunia
Poinsettia

BULBS TO PLANT IN AUGUST

Calla-Lily (white)
Cyrtanthus

Freesia
Lachenalia
Oxalis

SEEDS TO PLANT IN AUGUST

African Violet
Ageratum
Aster, China
Bellis
Calendula
Centaurea
Celosia
Cineraria
Coleus
Cyclamen

Didiscus
Dimorphotheca
Gypsophila
Marigold
Mignonette
Nasturtium
Nemesia
Nerium
Nicotiana
Pansy

Phlox Drummondi
Primula
Salvia
Schizanthus
Snapdragon
Stock
Sweet Alyssum
Sweet Pea

9. September

September is the month of great promise in a home greenhouse. There are open blooms on early chrysanthemums, but mostly buds to tell of the floral display soon to come. Robust seedlings of cineraria, calceolaria, and cyclamen, brought in from outdoor frames, breathe a hint of spring, and poinsettias, carefully placed away from any evening illumination of patio and street lights, whisper of Christmas. But not all is for the future. Abutilons bloom abundantly; aphelandra sends up waxy, golden bracts; and celosias lift plumes in the rich colors of a Persian carpet. For evening fragrance there is that favorite species orchid, *Brassavola nodosa*.

Now begins one of the busiest months in the greenhouse year. It is a time for many small but vitally important chores like final checking of the heating system and removal of summer shading. The only major project is to bring potted plants back into the greenhouse before frost, but fringe duties add up to a capacity schedule. Besides, the outdoor fall planting of hardy perennials, evergreens, and spring-flowering bulbs is a full-time September job for most gardeners.

UPKEEP, HEALTH, AND WELFARE

The subject of pest control is never a pleasant one, yet it has to be dealt with if you are to achieve success with your home greenhouse. *Under Glass* readers who filled out my questionnaire indicated that pest control was a serious problem. September, the real beginning of another season of greenhouse gardening, is the time to begin an effective pest-control program.

Preventive maintenance has always been my approach to a pest-free greenhouse. Proper culture, prompt removal of all debris, and good ventilation form my line of defense against plant pestilence. In addition, once every three months I replace one Shell No-Pest Strip in my 10 x 20 greenhouse with a fresh one. With one of these hung out of sight among taller plants, I find that it completely eliminates all problems with aphids, mealybugs, cyclamen mite, red spider-mite, scale, and thrips. I would not use a No-Pest Strip in a room where food is prepared or eaten, or in a room where a cat or dog wearing a flea collar lives.

Before I discovered the convenience and efficacy of the No-Pest Strips, I backed up constant watchfulness for insects by using a sprayer filled with houseplant pesticide for quick jobs, and by dipping plants in a pail of insecticide to combat serious infestations.

Several *Under Glass* readers also report excellent pest control with the Shell No-Pest Strips. A grower in Oregon, for example, reported that one is ample for his 9 x 12 greenhouse. A woman in New Hampshire wrote that mealybugs had been her greatest problem. When usual spraying failed, she went after the mealybugs one by one, plant by plant, with alcohol and a paintbrush.

A grower in Montana who specializes in begonias and geraniums uses only a houseplant aerosol for complete pest control. I have stopped using and advocating the use of aerosols owing to their environmental threat to ozone in the atmosphere. A Maine grower recommends nicotine smoke bombs instead of sprays, and uses these for control in two 24 x 14 foot greenhouses. I too have used these in the past, but have found the fumes devastating to begonias and ferns. An organic gardener in Illinois uses ladybugs and praying mantises to control harmful insects naturally. And a successful grower in Nebraska recommends monthly spraying with synthetic pyrethrin mixed in a battery-powered spray unit.

Another way to combat greenhouse insect pests is simply to bathe infected plants in soapy water, and then rinse well with clean water; repeat at five-day intervals. Organically safe Ced-o-flora (available from plant shops and garden centers) and Dr. Bronner's Peppermint Soap (sold at health-food stores) mixed with water and sprayed on plants are also recommended.

Labor Day Weekend. Feeding plants, as usual, comes first, but some are slowing down now—amaryllis, for example— and fertilizer should be withheld. Tender perennials like Jerusalem cherries, and annuals like celosias that you are growing for future greenhouse bloom, need regular biweekly

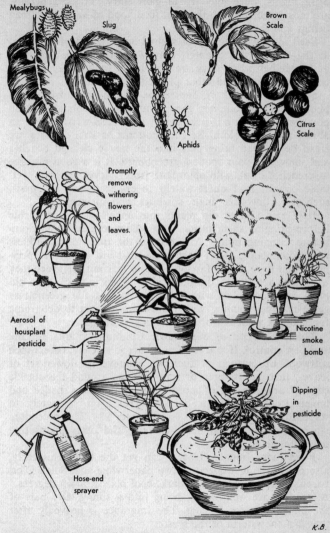

Mealybugs

Slug

Brown Scale

Citrus Scale

Aphids

Promptly remove withering flowers and leaves.

Aerosol of housplant pesticide

Nicotine smoke bomb

Hose-end sprayer

Dipping in pesticide

K.B.

FIGURE 5 *Greenhouse pests and how to control them.*

feeding. Pest control is all-important now, and with the first brisk nights, mice may try to gain entry. Traps, generally, are most effective, with the least likelihood of harm to human beings and family pets.

Seed sowing, especially of annual flowers, and others listed at the end of this chapter, may well go on this first part of September while days are still fairly long. Stake and tie chrysanthemums, and other plants that need it.

Second Weekend of September. Begin to move potted plants from the outdoor garden into the greenhouse. Clean pots well, scrubbing if necessary with a steel-wool pad or an abrasive kitchen cloth. Be sure bottoms as well as sides are clean before you bring pots into the newly cleaned benches and shelves of your spotless greenhouse. It is a good practice to drench the soil with chlordane (mix 1 level teaspoon wettable powder to 1 quart water) to eradicate any soil pests, such as earthworms, gnats, sowbugs, and springtails.

It is wise also to dip plants into an all-purpose pesticide before bringing them inside. Dip, allow to stand, and drain before bringing inside. And now is the time to be ruthless with your plants. Don't keep those that are ailing, or specimens that have grown far too large to warrant the space they will take. Sometimes the only thing to do is discard an old plant and start over with cuttings. Part of the greenhouse game is experimenting with plants new to you to determine for yourself what is worth occupying your space.

Third Weekend of September. Continue routine feeding and pest control. If you have not done so already, take 3-inch softwood tip cuttings of fuchsias. Remove the lower set of leaves, then insert three or four cuttings around the outside edge of a 3-inch pot of moist vermiculite. Keep shaded and moist. Roots will form quickly. Transplant separately to standard fuchsia potting soil (see Chapter 13). This procedure works also with geraniums, begonias, and other plants that have summered outdoors.

Plant more freesias. If you can get the bulbs this early, also put in the first dozen or two paperwhite and 'Soleil D'or' narcissus. Keep moist, in a dark, cool place (50-60 degrees). After they are well-rooted, bring into a sunny, airy part of the greenhouse for forcing. The fragrance is heavenly after that first snowstorm of the season.

Fourth Weekend of September. Continue moving-in operations, aiming at having inside the greenhouse everything that really matters by the end of the month. And if you have the space, here is an idea worth trying: Dig clumps of button chrysanthemums from the garden, cut off all blooms as soon as they are spent. Feed regularly. Provide full sun in an airy, moist atmosphere. New growth will give January bloom at a time when it is doubly appreciated. Afterwards cut back to an inch or two from the soil and place in a coldframe until planting-out time in spring.

FLOWERING PLANTS FOR SEPTEMBER

Abutilon	Clerodendrum	Lantana
Achimenes	Coleus	Marguerite
African Violet	Columnea	Orchid: Brassavola
Allamanda	Crassula	digbyana var. Fim-
Aphelandra	Crossandra	bripetala
Ardisia	Dipladenia	Orchid: Brassavola
Begonia	Episcia	nodosa
Beloperone	Euphorbia	Oxalis
Bougainvillea	Fuchsia	Pentas
Bouvardia	Gazania	Petunia
Browallia	Geranium	Punica
Cacti	Gloxinia	Rose
Caladium	Gypsophila	Salvia
Calla-Lily	Haemanthus	Smithiantha
Campanula	Hibiscus, Chinese	Solanum
Celosia	Impatiens	Spathiphyllum
Cestrum	Ixora	Sweet Alyssum
Chrysanthemum	Jacobinia	Tibouchina
Citrus	Jasminum	Tulbaghia

REPOTTING AND DIVIDING TO DO IN SEPTEMBER

African Violet	Ornithogalum
Lapeirousia	Primula
Orchid	Veltheimia

CUTTINGS TO MAKE IN SEPTEMBER

Abutilon	Crossandra
Azalea	Jasminum
Beloperone	Lantana
Crassula	Petunia

BULBS TO PLANT IN SEPTEMBER

Amaryllis
Anemone
Babiana
Calla-Lily (white)
Crocus

Cyrtanthus
Daffodil
Hyacinth
Iris, Dutch
Ixia

Lachenalia
Narcissus, Paper-
   white
Ornithogalum

SEEDS TO PLANT IN SEPTEMBER

African Violet
Aster, China
Calceolaria
Centaurea
Cineraria
Clarkia

Didiscus
Gloxinia
Godetia
Gypsophila
Marigold
Nasturtium
Nemesia

Phlox Drummondi
Salpiglossis
Salvia
Schizanthus
Snapdragon
Sweet Pea
Ursinia

10. *October*

Boxes of new plants, some untried varieties and some old-timers, arrive this month, along with bulbs for forcing—tulips, daffodils, paperwhites, and hyacinths. Moments in the greenhouse are precious indeed. Cascade chrysanthemums drape the north wall. In front, the garden bench is flanked on either side by a tree geranium in full bloom with radiant scarlet flowers. In the bench opposite a dozen young plants of king's crown *(Jacobinia carnea)* open brilliant pink, and the trumpets of dipladenia, twining on a trellis beyond, complete a rosy picture. In the north bench, pots of Christmas peppers, one plant several years old and trained as a standard, put on a holiday preview along with dwarf plume celosias and newly potted cuttings of wax begonias, coleus, and impatiens.

This delightful month of generally warm, sunny days, and cool, if not chilly, nights is a time when automatic heating, cooling, and ventilating systems are most appreciated and these need to be in first-class working order.

Clean-up of falling leaves and spent flowers is vital now because weather conditions may tend to encourage disease. You probably won't have to water as much or as often as you will later to keep soil evenly moist.

In most areas, all greenhouse shading can come off this month. Give the glass a polishing inside and out before late fall or early winter weather sets in to make this pleasant October task a miserable chore for a dreary November afternoon.

Be ready to pot up shipments of new plants, and spring-flowering bulbs for forcing. Lay in a plentiful supply of clean pots and flats, labels, and soil mixture ingredients.

Cross-section shows bulb pan with layer of pebbles for drainage, then soil, with bulb tips near surface.

Potted bulbs placed in trench outdoors for rooting period of 6 to 10 weeks.

Forcing may begin when green shoots show, and roots have formed.

FIGURE 6   *How to force spring-flowering bulbs.*

YOUR SOIL SERVICE DEPARTMENT

A good growing medium is the foundation for successful container gardening. I use vermiculite or milled sphagnum moss for all propagating work in my greenhouse and garden. Most of my plants are grown either in a simple mixture of equal parts garden loam, peat moss, and sand, or in a commercially prepared soil-less medium such as Jiffy-Mix, Redi-earth, Supersoil, or Pro-Mix.

A successful greenhouse gardener in Ohio substitutes Michigan peat for garden loam, using it in equal parts with Canadian peat moss and sand. Another grower uses the time-honored equal parts garden loam, peat moss, and sand, but mixes into each bushel a pint each of steamed bone meal and dried commercial sheep fertilizer. An *Under Glass* reader in Nebraska follows this recipe: 3 parts "good black dirt," 1 part sand and 2 of peat moss, plus a sprinkling of bone meal and powdered charcoal.

Every discussion about potting soil is supposed to detail pasteurization techniques. Confidentially, I have never been a soil sterilizing gardener, chiefly because it is too much trouble, but now there is an easy way to have a sterile growing medium. Use the Peat-Lite mix developed at Cornell University. Here is the recipe for mixing one peck:

Vermiculite (Terra-Lite)	4 quarts
Shredded sphagnum peat moss	4 quarts
20 per cent superphosphate (powdered)	1 teaspoon
Ground, dolomitic limestone	1 tablespoon

Plus either of the following (not both):

33 per cent ammonium nitrate	1 tablespoon
5-10-5 commercial fertilizer	4 tablespoons

Moisten this mixture well before using. Five to six weeks after potting plants in it, begin biweekly feedings with a house-plant fertilizer diluted according to manufacturer's directions.

First Weekend of October. After feeding and pest control, check on the drying-off of summer bulbs such as achimenes, caladiums, pink and yellow calla-lilies, and tuberous begonias.

This is a good time, and about the last chance, to make a flower forecast for your greenhouse. Decide whether you have all the plants you will need to put on the flower show you want from now until next spring. If in doubt, get out your catalogs. Order some new geraniums. Add winter-flowering tuberous-rooted begonias. Fatten up the bloom schedule for any time ahead that needs it. Get your order off this weekend, via air mail.

Second Weekend of October. Pot up spring-flowering bulbs for forcing. Of course, you will have crocuses, hyacinths, daffodils, tulips, and bulbous irises (Dutch, English, and Spanish). For fun, pot up some of the less common kinds that you probably have on hand for planting outdoors. Consider calochortus, chionodoxa, winter aconite, triteleia, muscari, puschkinia, snowdrops, and scillas. Start with a pot each of those that appeal to you. If performance proves them worth more space, you can increase your order next year.

When you purchase these dormant bulbs in autumn, they contain perfectly formed flower buds. Coolness, warmth, moisture, darkness, and light in the right degrees and at the right times will bring these hidden buds into glorious winter bloom. Use clay or plastic bulb pans and a mixture of equal parts garden loam, peat moss, and sand. Position bulbs so that the tips are near the surface, even protruding slightly. Moisten well. Then place in a dark, cool place, ideally a range of 35 to 50 degrees, for a rooting period of at least six to ten weeks. This may be in a coldframe, on the floor of an unheated garage, or simply in a trench outdoors. An old refrigerator with the thermostat set at about 45 degrees F. can be an excellent place for rooting pots of spring bulbs.

Wherever you place pots of bulbs for rooting, be sure that the growing medium is kept uniformly moist. Unless your bulbs were especially treated for Christmas bloom, do not try to force until after the holidays. Then bring a few pots each week to the greenhouse. A moist, sunny, airy atmosphere will bring out the best in them. After petals fade, keep soil moist, and provide sun or fluorescent light until danger of severe freezing is past, then plant out to a permanent place in the garden.

Third Weekend of October. Continue regular feeding and pest control. Remember, however, that many plants are going downhill at this season. Use your own judgment as to whether a plant needs the usual amount of fertilizer, a more diluted feeding, or none at all.

Bulb planting for forcing may continue this weekend. Inevitably, in a well-kept greenhouse, there will be less work to do now and more time for other pleasures. Read the latest gardening books and magazines. Attend a college football game.

Fourth Weekend of October. There is still time to plant bulbs for forcing, and in the garden outdoors in most climates. Toward the South where frosts may not yet have occurred, continue moving-in activities. Over a large part of the country this weekend may well find the greenhouse gardener with little to do beyond routine watering and clean-up. The rest of the time will be free to enjoy the fine flower show inside.

FLOWERING PLANTS FOR OCTOBER

Abutilon	Chrysanthemum	Jasminum
Acalypha	Citrus	Lantana
Achimenes	Clerodendrum	Orchid: Cattleya
African Violet	Coleus	'Enid Alba'
Aphelandra	Columnea	Orchid: Brassavola
Ardisia	Crassula	nodosa
Begonia	Crossandra	Oxalis
Beloperone	Dipladenia	Pentas
Bougainvillea	Episcia	Petunia
Bouvardia	Euphorbia	Punica
Browallia	Gazania	Rose
Cacti	Geranium	Salvia
Calendula	Gypsophila	Smithiantha
Camellia	Haemanthus	Solanum
Campanula	Hibiscus, Chinese	Spathiphyllum
Capsicum	Impatiens	Sweet Alyssum
Celosia	Ixora	Tibouchina
Cestrum	Jacobinia	Tulbaghia

REPOTTING AND DIVIDING TO DO IN OCTOBER

African Violet	Lily
Cyrtanthus	Orchids
Lapeirousia	Ornithogalum

CUTTINGS TO MAKE IN OCTOBER

Abutilon	Crassula
Azalea	Crossandra
Beloperone	Lantana

11. *November*

Late chrysanthemums, the elegant "spiders" and giant "footballs," reign this month. Pots and tubs brought along outdoors through the summer are grouped along the aisle and at the ends and behind the garden bench. Achimenes, tuberous begonias, and caladiums, ready to be dried off for dormancy, give way to this show, and make room for the more compact "button" mums at bench height.

But there's more. Scarlet, pink, and purple flowering sage plants, potted and rescued from frost, take on new life, and pots of lantana cuttings rooted in August add to the color festival. In a planter box beside my potting bench, sweet peas started in July and trained on a trellis form a fragrant camouflage for my garden trappings, and on a glass shelf behind the bench my treasure plant of bougainvillea 'Barbara Karst' puts on an early show. I check pots of amaryllis, brought in before frost and dried off, for signs of buds, and discover that in haste *Tulbaghia fragrans* has also been turned on its side to rest. This shock has brought two bloom stalks. Another season I did this to *Nerine falcata* and received from it the first flowers in five years.

Diminishing day-length is always felt this month. Go easy with the hose, and water early in the day so that excess moisture can evaporate by evening. Keep the glass clean, polishing to allow maximum entry of the waning rays. Space out potted plants to allow free air circulation, and put small plants in the best possible location for light.

Remove all dried foliage from summer-flowering bulbs, such as tuberous begonias, achimenes, and caladiums. Keep the roots nearly dry, and store at approximately 50 to 60 degrees.

ORGANIZE THE NECESSITIES

Every home greenhouse gardener needs a pleasant place to work and storage space for equipment. When the weather is warm enough, I take care of dividing and repotting outdoors (Chapter 4), but at this time of the year, my greenhouse potting bench is a favorite place. There I have plastic pails of soil ingredients (bulk quantities are stored in less valuable space in the garage), pots stacked by size along the back of the bench, and a shelf up high (so I will not swish the hose on it) for labels, handy reference books, and a Mason jar filled with packets of seeds I will be planting. This area is screened from the rest of the greenhouse by a redwood trellis covered with a passionflower vine. An extension speaker from the stereo in the house, a telephone, and a stool at comfortable height make work sessions here all the more enjoyable.

First Weekend of November. After feeding and pest control, there are a number of seeds that can be sown now. The list at the end of this chapter suggests some. Also, try calceolaria for May blooms on plants in 3-inch pots, hybrid gloxinias for a magnificent showing in March and April, and calendulas and candytuft for spring flowering.

Check early this month to be sure that no artificial light is reaching Christmas cactus and poinsettias between sundown and sunup; otherwise, holiday flowering may be delayed if not prevented entirely.

For roses in February, buy a half dozen dormant bushes early this month if you have room to force them. Pot each in a 12-inch clay pot or redwood tub. Keep evenly moist, and provide a pleasantly moist, airy, sunny atmosphere. Spray biweekly with an all-purpose rose pesticide. Fertilize biweekly as soon as new growth breaks. Early in May you can trim back the bushes and plant them outdoors for summer bloom. Or, simply move them into larger containers for decorating your outdoor living area.

November is also a good time to buy a few dormant clematis hybrids. Plant each in a 6- to 8-inch pot, and give the same good care you would any other flowering plant, a geranium, for example. The flowers you will get in the green-

FIGURE 7 *Home greenhouse potting bench and storage space.*

house in winter from a clematis will make it eminently worthwhile.

Second Weekend of November. Sow any of the seeds suggested last week. Also, devote some attention to making new cuttings, and to potting those taken earlier that have formed root systems. This weekend is practically last call for potting bulbs to be forced. Of course, Dutch hybrid amaryllis may not arrive until later in the month, but all hardy kinds like tulips, daffodils, hyacinths, and crocuses need to be in pots of soil by now.

Third Weekend of November. Feed anything in active growth, but go lightly, if at all, on all other plants. Pest control merits your usual attention, not that most pests thrive on the short days, but you have more time to stalk out pests now than you will have early in the year, or during the coming holidays. As part of this activity, pick up every pot. Clean it well on the outside and use a fork to cultivate the surface soil to fine tilth. Then groom the plant as if you were going to enter it in a spring flower show.

Fourth Weekend of November. Be sure that all tropicals—poinsettias and philodendrons, for example—are out of cold drafts. Check the alarm system (or install one).

Keep a roll of sturdy polyethylene plastic handy, also masking tape, in case panes are broken during a winter storm, or at any time when you cannot replace the glass immediately.

FLOWERING PLANTS FOR NOVEMBER

Abutilon	Chrysanthemum	Hibiscus, Chinese
Acalypha	Citrus	Impatiens
African Violet	Clerodendrum	Ixora
Amaryllis	Coleus	Jacobinia
Aphelandra	Columnea	Jasminum
Ardisia	Crassula	Lantana
Begonia	Crossandra	Mignonette
Beloperone	Cyclamen	Orchid: Cattleya
Bougainvillea	Cyrtanthus	'Barbara Dane'
Bouvardia	Didiscus	Orchid: Brassavola
Browallia	Dipladenia	nodosa
Cacti	Episcia	Oxalis
Calendula	Euphorbia	Pentas
Camellia	Geranium	Petunia
Capsicum	Gypsophila	Rose
Cestrum	Heliotrope	Salvia

FLOWERING PLANTS FOR NOVEMBER
[*Continued*]

Smithiantha	Spathiphyllum	Tulbaghia
Solanum	Sweet Alyssum	
Snapdragon	Sweet Pea	

REPOTTING AND DIVIDING TO DO IN NOVEMBER

African Violet	Orchids
Cyrtanthus	Ornithogalum
Lapeirousia	

CUTTINGS TO MAKE IN NOVEMBER

Azalea	Crassula
Beloperone	Crossandra

BULBS TO PLANT IN NOVEMBER

Amaryllis	Hyacinth
Crocus	Ixia
Daffodil	Tulip

SEEDS TO PLANT IN NOVEMBER

Achimenes	Godetia
African Violet	Nemesia
Clarkia	Sweet Pea

12. *December*

One morning early in the month we awaken to a sensation of unusual brightness in the house. This is due to the reflection of new snow that makes beautiful the forms of frosted plants that only last evening were forlorn and ugly in the gray cold. The boys and I can hardly wait to be outside, they to play in the snow, and I to step into the greenhouse. For me there is always a special moment as I stand in the warm, moist atmosphere, surrounded by the green lushness of growing plants and bursting flower buds, and look beyond to a landscape draped with ice and snow. Then, with renewed appreciation for my greenhouse, I turn to the pleasant routine of checking the plants.

The holiday spirit is apparent even in the greenhouse as poinsettias turn bracts to creamy yellow, dusty pink, and fiery red. Christmas peppers, begonias, cactus, Jerusalem cherries, chenille plant, and ardisia add to the festivity. Besides these traditional holiday plants, there will be amaryllis, azaleas, citrus, cyclamen, the first gloriously fragrant freesia blooms of the season, geraniums, paperwhites, possibly a few roses, snapdragons, and sprays of cymbidium orchids.

Aside from routine maintenance, December in a home greenhouse can be a calm month, with few demands. This is fortunate since Christmas activities tend to be overwhelming. Be sure that the glass is clean to admit all possible sunshine and that the heating and ventilating system is in A-1 condition. Go easy on watering and feeding. Use rooted cuttings, seedlings, and miniatures to plant bottle gardens for friends and yourself.

First Weekend of December. Feed plants in active growth and take care of pest control. Anemones and ranunculus that have been in a protected coldframe, or under the bench getting started, may be brought to sunlight and warmth. Start several containers of paperwhite narcissus into active growth for fragrant blooms at Christmas.

Start tubers of glory lily (gloriosa) for earliest spring

Use funnel to place growing medium in container.

Start with small plants and rooted cuttings.

Copper wire and slender stick are helpful tools.

Mold pleasing terrain with pliable stick.

Copper wire holds plant as it is positioned.

K. BOURKE

FIGURE 8 *How to plant a bottle garden.*

bloom. Tubers may be 8 to 10 inches long, so use large pots or tubs. Grow at a 60-degree nighttime temperature in a sunny, airy, moist atmosphere.

Second Weekend of December. Try to finish potting, re-potting, dividing, and staking now for the balance of the year.

When you take gift plants from the warmth of your green-house, protect them from the outside cold. Have your car well-heated before putting plants in it. In severe weather, or if you are giving tropicals that resent the slightest chill (poin-settias, for example), protect them with boxes, or cover them with several thicknesses of newspaper, carefully stapling the covers around the plants.

Sow tuberous begonia seeds now for an abundant crop of flowering-size seedlings for next summer. If you have time, there are a number of flower seeds to sow now for spring bloom. These include annual baby's-breath (gypsophila), larkspur, sweet peas, and stock. You may defer this planting until the fourth weekend of December, but the second is preferable.

Third Weekend of December. If you have extra time, feed plants in active growth with a half-strength solution. But take it easy, this is the Christmas season. Enjoy it. Maintain your greenhouse with the least possible care. Be sure the heating system is working well and keep soil evenly moist. Otherwise, take time to enjoy looking at your flowers and sharing them with friends.

Pest control *may* require attention, no matter how busy you are with Christmas shopping and decorations. Above all, do not neglect calceolarias and cinerarias. Aphids have a way of infesting them overnight with damaging results.

Fourth Weekend of December. You can read your January gardening magazines now and order catalogs from firms with whom you are not listed. Catch up on pest and clean-up de-tail that may have been neglected earlier in the month. If any dirty pots, flats, or other equipment has accumulated, clean and store it now before the start of the new year.

After Christmas, your local florist may be glad to let you have the pick of his leftover poinsettias since those not sold must be discarded to make way for new crops. If your green-house is warm, humid, and well-lighted, poinsettias will be colorful for at least another eight weeks. Most florists are glad to let the plants find a good home; you may have to pay for the clay pots, or promise to return them, but otherwise, this is an inexpensive way to increase your midwinter flower show. And a pleasant way to end the year, satisfied that you have saved some tropical plants from a frozen compost heap.

FLOWERING PLANTS FOR DECEMBER

Abutilon
Acalypha
African Violet
Amaryllis
Ardisia
Azalea
Begonia
Beloperone
Bougainvillea
Bouvardia
Browallia
Cacti
Calendula
Camellia
Capsicum
Cestrum
Chrysanthemum
Citrus
Coleus
Columnea
Crossandra
Cyclamen
Cyrtanthus
Didiscus

Djpladenia
Echeveria
Episcia
Euphorbia
Exacum
Felicia
Freesia
Gardenia
Geranium
Gerbera
Gypsophila
Heliotrope
Hibiscus, Chinese
Hyacinth
Impatiens
Ixora
Jacobinia
Jasminum
Lantana
Marigold
Mignonette
Myosotis
Narcissus

Orchid: Cymbidium
 'Fairy Wand'
Orchid: Brassavola
 nodosa
Orchid: Oncidium
 splendidum
Orchid: Oncidium
 tigrinum
Oxalis
Pansy
Pentas
Petunia
Poinsettia
Rose
Salvia
Smithiantha
Snapdragon
Solanum
Stevia
Sweet Alyssum
Sweet Pea
Tulbaghia
Tulip

REPOTTING AND DIVIDING TO DO IN DECEMBER

African Violet
Orchids

CUTTINGS TO MAKE IN DECEMBER

Beloperone
Crassula
Crossandra

BULBS TO PLANT IN DECEMBER

Amaryllis

SEEDS TO PLANT IN DECEMBER

African Violet
Begonia
Candytuft
Centaurea

Godetia
Lobelia
Nemesia
Nierembergia

Petunia (Double
   Grandiflora)
Sweet Alyssum

13. *The Best Flowers for a Flowering Greenhouse*

The 134 plants described in this chapter have been selected for their free-flowering habits and all-around desirability for a home greenhouse. The phrase "nighttime temperature" refers generally to that time of year when the greenhouse is heated artificially. The term "evenly moist" means pleasant to the touch; not bone dry or dripping wet. Keeping soil evenly moist requires more frequent watering during the long, sunny days of spring and summer than it does in the short, often dark days of fall and winter. Rooting and seed-starting mediums of vermiculite or milled sphagnum moss have been recommended for most plants, but other favorites such as clean, sharp sand, or equal parts peat moss and sand may be used. If you do not have access to the leaf mold recommended for some soil mixtures, substitute vermiculite. Perlite may be used in place of sand.

Abutilon

Pendant, bell flowers in lavender, pink, red, salmon, white, or yellow, almost all year on new growth. Soft-hairy leaves shaped like those of the maple, hence, "flowering maple."

CULTURE:

Nighttime temperature 45-55 degrees. Soil: equal parts garden loam, peat moss, and sand. Keep evenly moist. Plants do well outdoors in summer in partially shaded location. Move into greenhouse before danger of frost, probably in September, and cut back to induce new growth. Repot in late winter or spring. Pinch back growing tips to encourage branching. Provide full sun in winter, a little shade the rest of the year.

PROPAGATION:

Root cuttings in September and October to have vigorous, young plants for winter and spring bloom. Sow seeds of hybrid strains in March, April, or May, for bloom beginning the following winter.

Acacia

Clusters of fluffy, yellow flowers in February, March, and April. Small shrub or tree easily kept to 5 feet or less in greenhouse.

CULTURE:

Nighttime temperature 45-55 degrees. Soil: equal parts garden loam, peat moss, and sand. Keep evenly moist. Feed biweekly from March to July. Prune back in June and repot every two or three years. Acacias need a sunny, airy, moist atmosphere in the greenhouse. Keep outdoors in summer in partially shaded place. Return to greenhouse before danger of hard freezing in autumn. Do not subject to dry heat inside at any time.

PROPAGATION:

Take cuttings in June or July; insert in moist mixture of equal parts peat moss and sand; provide high humidity by covering with polyethylene, but keep in full shade. Seeds planted in March or April, ⅛ inch deep in moist peat moss and sand, will germinate readily in warm place, but flowering may not occur for two years or more. Flowering-size plants of *Acacia baileyana* and *A. longifolia floribunda* are available from Logee's Greenhouses (Appendix).

Acalypha

Flowers bright red (*A. hispida*) or pinkish (*A.h. alba*) in long (to 12 inches or more), slender, drooping spikes. October to April.

CULTURE:

Nighttime temperature 60-65 degrees. Soil: equal parts garden loam, peat moss, and sand. Keep evenly moist. Provide full sun November through March.

PROPAGATION:

Take 4-inch tip cuttings February to July; insert in moist vermiculite; provide warmth (70-75 degrees), high humidity, and shade.

Achimenes

Flowers blue, crimson, lavender, pink, purple, violet, white, or yellow, from June until October. Showy for baskets, boxes, and pots. Varieties for baskets include 'Adelaide,' 'Brilliant,' 'Cattleya,' 'Dentoniana' or 'Giant Pansy,' 'Escheriana' or 'Carmine Queen,' *longiflora* 'Major,' 'Purple King,' and 'Royal Purple.'

16 *A hanging basket of achimenes in full bloom is one of the rewards of having a greenhouse. Scaly rhizomes planted in late winter or early spring yield a nonstop flower show from June until autumn.* AUTHOR

CULTURE:

Nighttime temperature 55 degrees minimum, but 70 or 80 degrees while seeds or scaly rhizomes are being started. Provide semisun in spring; bright, open shade in summer. Plant the scaly rhizomes about 1 inch apart and 1 inch deep from February to April in equal parts garden loam, peat moss, sand, and leaf mold; or try pure unmilled sphagnum moss and feed weekly with a diluted liquid houseplant fertilizer like fish emulsion. Pinch out the growing tips of young plants to encourage branching. Keep evenly moist from planting time until about October when moisture is withheld until the tops die off. Afterwards, set the containers in a dark place with a temperature range of 50 to 60 degrees and leave there nearly dry until time to start again.

PROPAGATION:

Each scaly rhizome multiplies into several every year. Achimenes seeds planted in November in warmth and high humidity on moist vermiculite or screened sphagnum moss will provide blooming plants the following summer.

African Violet (*Saintpaulia* species)

Blue, lavender, pink, purple, red, rose, violet, or white flowers all year, but especially for fall, winter, and spring in the greenhouse.

CULTURE:

Nighttime temperature 60-65 degrees. Soil: equal parts garden loam, peat moss, and sand; or, use a commercially prepared medium labeled for African Violets. Keep evenly moist. Feed every two or three weeks. Use water at room temperature, never icy cold. Violets ship well, and outstanding varieties may be purchased by mail from specialists (Appendix) whenever the weather is warm. Plants received in 2¼-inch pots in September and moved into 4-inch containers will give a beautiful flower show from December to May. In a warm, moist, airy atmosphere African violets can take some full sun in late fall and winter, but the balance of the year they need bright, open shade. Keep yellowing leaves and spent flowers picked off.

17 It takes only a half dozen healthy African violets to assure having a greenhouse that is never entirely without flowers. The one shown is the newly popular miniature called 'Pixie Blue' which is an ideal subject for cultivating in a small hanging basket.
AUTHOR

PROPAGATION:

Divide multiple-crowned plants any time. Vigorous leaves, not the oldest and not the youngest on the plant, with 1 inch of petiole (the leaf-stalk) will root readily in moist vermiculite; when a cluster of new plants shows around the base, divide and pot separately; blooming plants are possible by this method in six months. Sow seeds any time on moist vermiculite or milled sphagnum moss; keep moderately warm (about 72 degrees) and out of direct sun; first blooms in six to eight months.

Agapanthus

Blue or white flowers in spring and summer; vigorous leaves similar to amaryllis of ornamental value for contrast with plants of more rounded form and texture.

CULTURE:

Nighttime temperature 50-60 degrees. Soil: equal parts garden loam, peat moss, and sand. Keep on dry side from September to February. Water more freely from March to August and feed biweekly. A plant in a 12-inch pot or tub will need repotting only once every three or four years.

PROPAGATION:

Divide large specimens in February or March. For a plentiful supply, sow seeds in warm (70-75 degrees), sunny location; first blooms in three years.

Ageratum

Blue, pink, or white flowers from February to May.

CULTURE:

Nighttime temperature 60 degrees. Soil: equal parts garden loam, peat moss, and sand. Keep evenly moist and feed biweekly from mid-January on. Needs sunny, moist, airy atmosphere.

PROPAGATION:

Sow seeds in August or take cuttings from plants growing in the garden, to provide winter-blooming plants. Cuttings made from stock plants in February will reach blooming size by late April or May. Also, seeds sown in February will yield spring-blooming plants.

Allamanda

A climber with handsome, leathery, evergreen foliage. Trumpet-shaped golden yellow flowers from June to September.

18 *Allamanda has glorious, golden trumpet flowers and may be trained as a shrub or vine.* TOM EPHREM

CULTURE:

Nighttime temperature 60-70 degrees. Soil: equal parts garden loam, peat moss, and sand. Keep evenly moist and feed biweekly from April to September. Keep soil on dry side from October to March. To keep a convenient size, prune as necessary in January, February, or early March.

PROPAGATION:

Take 3-inch cuttings of previous year's growth in February, March, or April; root in vermiculite or mixture of moist peat moss and sand; keep in temperature range of 75-80 degrees; provide high humidity and shade.

19 *Amaryllis like this South African hybrid give spectacular bloom at any time from autumn to late spring.* JACKSON & PERKINS

Amaryllis

Crimson, pink, scarlet, or white lilylike flowers from November to May. Leathery strap-shaped leaves attractive all year except in fall.

CULTURE:

Nighttime temperature range of 60-65 degrees, except newly opened flowers will last longer at 50-55 degrees. Pot amaryllis when available, usually in fall and winter, in a mixture of equal parts garden·loam, peat moss, and sand. Keep barely moist and on the cool side (between 50-60 degrees) until rooting occurs, then bring to the top of the bench where the temperature is warmer. Flowering will occur within a few weeks. Feed biweekly from time flower buds show until about September.

There have been all kinds of detailed schedules published for growing amaryllis. I have a collection of approximately fifty South African and Dutch hybrids that I grow around the year with practically no trouble at all. Here is my no-bother schedule: (All were received originally in the fall of the year, and I potted each in a 6-inch pot. They bloomed at various times following the original planting, and afterwards I kept them in warmth and full sun, with nicely moist soil at all times and biweekly feeding.) In June each year I set all of them on a brick terrace at the north side of my house where they are fully exposed to the elements, excepting only full sun at midday. In the absence of regular rainfall, they are watered about twice a week, sometimes becoming very dry between these waterings. I feed once every two weeks, and beginning the first of September I withhold water and feeding. At that time the pots are turned on their sides. In about three weeks the leaves begin to wither, and I cut them all off. The pots are moved under the benches of the greenhouse well ahead of frost. After a dormancy period of about eight weeks I set all fifty pots on top of the benches, some at the cool end of the greenhouse where nighttime temperatures are about 50-55 degrees, and some toward the other end in a 60 to 68 range. They are kept nicely moist, and as soon as leaves or flower buds begin to show, feeding is resumed. That's all there is to it. From this number of bulbs I have some amaryllis in bloom from Thanksgiving until May. There are those who say that the bulbs must be dried off completely and repotted every autumn, but I have not found this necessary. I repot only every other year, and sometimes every third year, keeping the plants in 8-inch pots at the largest and adding only a little new soil each time.

Anemone

Blue, pink, purple, red, or white flowers in February, March, and April.

CULTURE:

Nighttime temperature 45-55 degrees. In September, pot corms 2 inches deep and 2 inches apart in a mixture of equal parts garden loam, peat moss, and sand. Set under the bench until growth starts.

PROPAGATION:

Seeds of hybrid strains planted in April, May, or June will give bloom the following February and March. These flowers probably will be larger and of better quality than those grown from corms. Transplant first to 2¼-inch pots, and keep shaded, cool, and moist all summer. Move to individual 4-inch pots in September.

Anemones are among the more troublesome flowering greenhouse plants, owing to the necessity of planting every year, watching for first growth, then moving to the top part of the bench, later providing some means of support for the weak stems and then drying off following flowering and storing nearly dry for the summer. However, anyone who admires the incomparable flower colors is willing to expend the effort to grow them.

Anthurium

Leathery spathes or "flowers" of coral, pink, red, or white, lasting for many weeks, and appearing from March to August.

CULTURE:

Nighttime temperature 65 degrees. Soil: equal parts shredded osmunda fiber, leaf mold, and unmilled sphagnum moss with a generous sprinkling of coarse sand or perlite. Water frequently, enough to keep the medium nicely moist. Anthuriums need tropical warmth and high humidity at all times, and bright light but no direct sunlight. The species *A. andreanum* and *A. scherzerianum* and their hybrids are the kinds grown for flowers. Some other kinds are grown only for showy foliage. In one home greenhouse where most of the space was devoted to orchids, I saw a delightful ground planting that featured anthuriums. These were grown in a small bed of leaf mold and sand, with a handsome piece of Oriental statuary as a focal point for the small garden. The owner told me it was not unusual to have color from the anthuriums almost all year and that they required no attention whatever. If yours is a tropical greenhouse, anthuriums deserve a place in it.

PROPAGATION:

Sow seeds in March or April in a mixture of milled sphagnum moss and sand; keep moist, in high humidity, and at 75-80 degrees.

Aphelandra

Striking cones of yellow, waxy bracts above handsome foliage, appearing in September, October, and November.

CULTURE:

Nighttime temperature 55-65 degrees. Soil: equal parts garden loam, leaf mold, peat moss, and sand. Keep evenly moist. Provide semisun in winter, partial shade through warm months. Feed biweekly in spring and summer. Check undersides of leaves frequently for red-spider mite and mealybug.

PROPAGATION:

In March, April, or May insert 4-inch tip cuttings in vermiculite; keep warm (70-80 degrees), moist, and shaded.

20 *Aphelandra or zebra plant has strikingly variegated golden-and-green leaves, each stem crowned in season by a long-lasting, waxy, golden bract from which relatively insignificant white flowers are borne. Never let this plant dry out.* AUTHOR

Ardisia

Bright red berries for cheerful color all through fall, winter, and spring. The foliage of this small shrub is glossy, leathery, and evergreen.

CULTURE:

Nighttime temperature 55-65 degrees. Soil: equal parts garden loam, sand, and peat moss. Water freely and feed biweekly from March to August. Keep on dry side from September to February. In March, prune as necessary to keep a nice shape. Repot every second or third spring. Ardisia is an excellent, carefree, permanent greenhouse plant.

PROPAGATION:

Sow seeds in moist soil and warmth (75 degrees) in March, April, or May. Cuttings may be rooted at the same time of year in similar conditions.

Aster, China

Blue, lavender, pink, rose, scarlet, white, or yellow flowers in spring or summer.

CULTURE:

Nighttime temperature 50-55 degrees. Soil: two parts garden loam to one part each of sand and peat moss. Keep evenly moist, feed biweekly as soon as growth becomes active.

PROPAGATION:

Sow seeds in April or May for August and September bloom. For this crop, I leave the pots or flats outdoors in a frame of peat moss, and bring them into the greenhouse for the first show of fall flowers. Seeds sown from July to October will yield January to April flowers of high quality in a sunny, airy greenhouse. They will need four extra hours of light every night, however, from seedflat stage to nearly-open beds. You can provide this by installing one reflector with a 60-watt incandescent bulb over every 4 or 5 feet of bench space. Use an automatic timer to turn lights on every day at 5 P.M., and off at 10 P.M.

Azalea

Crimson, lavender, pink, rose, salmon, or white flowers from December to April.

CULTURE:

Nighttime temperature 45-65 degrees. Soil: two parts acid peat moss (preferably German, but Canadian is acceptable) to one part sand. Keep evenly moist. Feed biweekly, from January to August. Provide a cool, moist atmosphere, sunny in winter, but shady in other seasons. To start with an azalea,

21 *A well-budded azalea purchased from a florist in autumn or early winter will give weeks if not months of bloom in a home greenhouse.* HORT-PIX

buy a plant beginning to open the first of many buds at a local florist. This will give several weeks of greenhouse color. After flowering, repot and prune to shape. Place outdoors in a cool, shaded, moist location from June to September. Before frost time, move to coldframe or cool under-bench area of greenhouse. Any time after about eight weeks move plant to top of bench where there is more warmth and light. Azaleas need an acid soil; if the water in your area is alkaline, feed occasionally with an iron chelate like Sequestrene, following manufacturer's directions.

PROPAGATION:

Sow seeds from January to March on surface of moist peat moss and sand; provide temperature of 55-65 degrees and high humidity. Take 3-inch tip cuttings from June to November; insert in moist peat moss and sand; provide bottom heat, high humidity, and keep out of direct sun.

Begonia

Flowers all year in all colors except blue. There are thousands of different kinds from which to choose. Every flowering greenhouse should have at least a dozen semperflorens (wax or everblooming) begonias, plus specimen plants from two or three other classes to add diversity of leaf and flowering habit. If your greenhouse is shaded and cool in summer, fill it with summer-flowering tuberous hybrids; otherwise, start the tubers in warmth from February to April, but grow

22 *Rieger begonias like 'Aphrodite Rose' may be cultivated in pots or hanging baskets for nonstop bloom almost all year.* AUTHOR

23   *Rex begonias are treasured for their richly colored and variegated leaves which, besides green, may be silver, brown, or burgundy with accents of pink or chartreuse.* AUTHOR

outdoors in warm weather. The named varieties suggested here have been selected on the basis of a long flowering season and all-around good performance in a home greenhouse; kinds useful in hanging baskets are followed by "hb." (In addition to those suggested in the lists, the Rieger hybrids are outstanding for blooms most of the year.)

24 Begonias vary in size from miniatures you can cup in your hand to giants 8 feet tall. Excepting one hanging basket of Episcia dianthiflora *(upper right), this greenhouse, which belongs to Mr. and Mrs. Edward Thompson, is filled entirely with different begonias which provide colorful foliage and flowers every day of the year.* BILL MULLIGAN

Semperflorens	*Rhizomatous*	*Cheimantha Hybrids*
'Aloha'	*bowerae*	(Flowers November
'Ballet'	'Cleopatra'	to March)
Butterfly hybrids	'Joe Hayden'	'Carolina'
'Carol'	'Ricky Minter'	'Christmas White'
'Cinderella Rose'		'Dark Marina'
'New Hampshire'		'Lady Mac'
'Pink Camellia' (hb)	*Foliage Beauties*	'Marjorie Gibbs'
'Pink Pearl'	*masoniana* (Iron	'Red Solfheim'
'Pink Wonder'	Cross)	
'South Pacific'	Rex hybrids	
'Spun Rose'		
'Thimbleberry'		

Hiemalis Hybrids	*Cane or Angelwing*
'Altrincham Pink'	'Anna Christine' (hb)
'Apricot Beauty'	'Corallina de Lucerna'
'Emily Clibran'	'Laura Engelbert' (hb)
'Emita'	'Lenore Olivier' (hb)
'Exquisite'	*limmingheiana* (hb)
'Man's Favourite'	*odorata alba* ((fragrant)
'Marietta'	'Pink Parade' (hb)
'The President'	'Tea Rose' (fragrant)
'Snowdrop'	

CULTURE:

Nighttime temperature 60-70 degrees (except 50-60 for hiemalis hybrids). Soil: equal parts garden loam, peat moss, and sand. Keep evenly moist. Feed biweekly, but withhold from tuberous types, including the hiemalis hybrids, during dormant season. When hiemalis and summer-flowering tuberous types finish flowering, withhold water and store nearly dry in a moderate temperature (50 degrees) until replanting time. Any fibrous-rooted begonia (except rhizomatous types) can be cut back freely following a period of heavy flowering, and new growth will rise with a new flower crop. Repot about once a year, from January to September. Rhizomatous begonias bloom naturally in winter and spring; they are best divided (if too large) and repotted from March to June.

PROPAGATION:

Sow seeds from December to June in warmth (about 70 degrees), on the surface of a moist, sterile medium such as vermiculite or milled sphagnum moss. Begonia seeds are infinitesimal, but they have amazing stamina; it is vital to success that newly planted seeds and young seedlings be protected from hot, dry air, and that the growing medium be evenly moist at all times. Propagate the hiemalis hybrids by dividing the surface bulbils into clusters of not less than five at repotting time in late summer or early fall, or by rooting tip cuttings of new growth in autumn. Stem cuttings 3 to 6 inches long of fibrous-rooted begonias can be rooted easily from January to September in moist vermiculite; provide shade and humidity while roots are forming. When the cheimantha hybrids let up flowering in March, cut back to an inch or two from the soil; new growth will show quickly, and cuttings made from it will form strong plants for the following winter's bloom.

Bellis

Pink, rose, or white flowers in February, March, April, and May. Usually called English daisy.

CULTURE:

Nighttime temperature 45-50 degrees. Provide sunny, airy, moist atmosphere.

PROPAGATION:

Sow seeds in August for bloom the following late winter and spring. Treat as annual except in climate with summer weather cool enough for the old plants to survive.

Beloperone

Brick-red, salmon, or chartreuse bracts all year. The popular "shrimp plant."

CULTURE:

Nighttime temperature 55-65 degrees. Soil: equal parts garden loam, sand, and peat moss. Keep evenly moist. Full sun
in winter will promote heavy flowering. Prune to shape any
time. Beloperone will tolerate all kinds of neglect and still
bloom constantly. I have seen it 8 feet tall, espaliered to the
roof of a lean-to greenhouse, but it may be used equally well
in a small hanging basket. This is a foolproof flowering plant
for a moderate to warm greenhouse.

PROPAGATION:

Cuttings root easily in warm, moist growing medium at any
time.

25   *Bougainvillea may be trained along the walls and roof of a
home greenhouse to form a natural canopy of foliage for shade,
with flowers in season, or you can dwarf it by pruning and cramp-
ing the roots in a small pot, bonsai-style.* WARD LINTON

Bougainvillea

Bronze, pink, or red bracts off and on all year. In my survey of home greenhouse gardeners across the country, bougainvillea rated as one of the most popular plants. My own specimen of 'Barbara Karst' grows in a 5-inch pot, is trimmed to less than 12 inches every spring, and summered outdoors on a shelf in full glaring sunlight. It dries out at times, but blooms constantly from early fall until late spring when I prune it back and place it outdoors again. Few plants can equal this performance.

CULTURE:

Nighttime temperature 55-65 degrees. Soil: equal parts garden loam, peat moss, and sand. Feed biweekly.

PROPAGATION:

Three-inch tip cuttings root readily from April to June in a moist, shaded place.

Bouvardia

Pink, red, or white flowers from September to February.

CULTURE:

Nighttime temperature 55-65 degrees. Soil: equal parts garden loam, peat moss, and sand. Keep evenly moist. Cut back in late winter or spring after flowering. Keep on dry side until you want to encourage new growth for making cuttings.

PROPAGATION:

Root tip cuttings in March, April, or May; keep moist and at about 65 degrees. Later, pinch out growing tips occasionally up to September 1 to encourage branching.

Bromeliads

The pineapple family is rich in plant material for the home greenhouse. There are numerous generic names, but all are

26 *Bromeliads are so richly varied, it takes only a dozen different ones to transform an ordinary collection of plants into an exotic garden. In this greenhouse the bromeliads are grouped in a ground bed with pieces of rock so that they appear to be growing wild.* AUTHOR

grouped commonly under the term "bromeliad." Seven recommended kinds that give year-round foliage interest and seasonal flower beauty: *Aechmea fasciata* 'Silver King,' *Ananas comosus variegatus, Cryptanthus bromelioides tricolor, Guzmania lingulata* hybrids, *Neoregelia carolinae tricolor, Tillandsia lindeni,* and *Vriesea splendens.*

CULTURE:

Nighttime temperature 60-70 degrees. Soil: equal parts garden loam, peat moss, leaf mold, and sand; or unmilled sphagnum moss. Keep moist by filling the vase formed by the leaf rosette with water, letting some run off into the growing medium. Provide summer shade and humidity in all seasons.

PROPAGATION:

Remove offsets that start at the base of parent plant, usually following the production of flowers; root in moist vermiculite or sphagnum moss in warmth (75-85 degrees), high humidity, and shade. Some bromeliads die after they have flowered, but not before sending up new shoots to replace the old.

Browallia

Blue, purple, or white flowers from September to June. Recommended named varieties: 'Blue Bells' (2-inch sky-blue flowers on 10-inch plants), 'Silver Bells' (snowy white 1-inch flowers on 8-inch plants), and 'Sapphire' (dark blue, white-eyed flowers on 12-inch plants).

CULTURE:

Nighttime temperature 50-60 degrees. Soil: equal parts garden loam, peat moss, and sand. Keep evenly moist. Feed biweekly. Provide sunny, moist atmosphere. Pinch out growing tips several times early in season to encourage branching. This plant is a tender perennial that may be kept from year to year by cutting back and repotting following a period of heavy flowering.

PROPAGATION:

Sow seeds from March to June in moist vermiculite or milled sphagnum moss; provide warmth (65-75 degrees) and high humidity. Transplant later, four or five seedlings to an 8-inch hanging basket, or pot of similar size. Tip cuttings made in February or March and rooted in moist vermiculite, warmth, and high humidity will provide flowering plants for outdoor container gardens in summer.

27   *Odd and rare cacti are the specialty of grower Paul Bosley, Jr. Baskets of flowering ivy-leaf geraniums, trailing verbena, and black-eyed-Susan vine hang from the roof.* ALUMINUM GREEN-HOUSES

Cacti

The cactus family can bring all-year interest and seasonal flower color to any greenhouse. There are countless kinds from which to choose. Here are twelve, available in this country by mail at reasonable prices, and all outstanding as flowering plants:

Desert Cacti

Aporocactus flagelliformis
Chamaecereus silvestris
Lobivia famatimensis
Lobivopsis Paramount hybrids
Notocactus haselbergi
Rebutia kupperiana

Jungle Cacti

Aporophyllum 'Lawrence' and 'Temple Glow'
Disophyllum 'Christmas Red'
Epiphyllum hybrids (orchid cacti)
Rhipsalidopsis 'Crimson Giant'
Schlumbergera bridgesi and *S. gaertneri*
Zygocactus bicolor and 'Mme. Ganna Walska'

CULTURE:

Nighttime temperature 60-70 degrees. Soil for desert cacti: equal parts garden loam, peat moss, and sand; keep on dry side. Soil for jungle cacti: equal parts garden loam, peat moss, leaf mold, and sand; keep evenly moist, allowing to approach dryness occasionally; keep schlumbergera and zygocactus almost dry from August to October. Provide full sun for desert cacti all year (partial shade in summer is fine); jungle cacti will benefit from filtered shade in late spring and summer. Feed all cacti biweekly from February to August; withhold food from September to January. Repot when plants are rootbound, from February to June.

PROPAGATION:

Make stem cuttings from March to June; allow cut parts to callous over, then insert in barely moist sand. Some cacti have offsets around the base of the old plant that may be removed and potted separately from March to June. Seeds sown from February to June and kept warm and moist yield interesting new plants.

Caladium

Outstanding foliage in colors of bronze, chartreuse, crimson, ivory, emerald, pink, rose, salmon, scarlet, and white, from April to September.

CULTURE:

Nighttime temperature 60-70 degrees. Soil: equal parts garden loam, peat moss, and sand. Start tubers in deep flat of moist vermiculite in February, March, or April. Keep barely moist until growth becomes apparent, then water freely and begin to feed biweekly. Allow four months from dormant tuber to a plant in full foliage. Transplant when well-rooted, one to a 6-inch pot, or three to a 10-inch container. Caladiums grow well in sun or shade. In active growth they need tropical warmth, humidity, and abundant moisture. In September withhold fertilizer and begin to water less. Finally, let the soil go almost completely dry. Store tubers for the winter in a temperature range of 50-60 degrees.

PROPAGATION:

Divide large clumps at repotting time.

28   *Calceolaria, the pocketbook plant, produces a vivid display of flowers in winter and spring from seeds started the previous spring or summer.* AUTHOR

Calceolaria

Pouch- or pocketbook-shaped flowers in brilliant orange, red, or yellow, spotted or tigered in contrasting color, from February to May.

CULTURE:

Nighttime temperature 45-55 degrees. Soil: equal parts garden loam, peat moss, and sand. Keep evenly moist; avoid severe dryness and excess moisture at all times. Provide sunny, moist, airy, cool atmosphere. Watch closely for aphids on new growth and spray if necessary. Discard plants after flowering.

PROPAGATION:

Sow seeds in June in coolness (50 degrees is ideal) to have specimen plants the following February, March, and April. Seeds sown in September will give 4-inch plants the following April and May. In climates where summer heat is severe,

29 Calendula, the pot-marigold of herbalists, yields wonderful flowers for cutting in winter and spring; an annual, easily grown from seeds. AUTHOR

calceolarias are best started in late August or September. Sow calceolaria seeds on moist vermiculite or milled sphagnum moss in a large bulb pan; keep as cool as possible (my basement floor is the coolest place I have in the summer). Seedlings need bright light and evenly moist soil; protect from dry heat. Feed weekly with a very diluted liquid houseplant fertilizer. When large enough to handle, transplant to 2¼-inch pots; as soon as roots fill this container, move to 3's or 4's; by December or January the plants will be ready for 5- or 6-inch containers.

Calendula

Orange or yellow daisy flowers from October to May. Recommended varieties for greenhouse culture: 'Sensation' or 'Campfire,' 'Lemon King Select,' 'Ball Orange Improved,' and 'Ball Gold.'

CULTURE:

Nighttime temperature 45-55 degrees (a warmer atmosphere will promote rank growth at the expense of good flower quality). Soil: equal parts garden loam, peat moss, and sand. Keep evenly moist. Feed biweekly with a fertilizer low in nitrogen content, 5-15-15, for example. Provide sunny, cool atmosphere. Calendula foliage may be attacked by powdery mildew if the greenhouse is damp and there is not good air circulation; if the disease occurs, spray every week with wettable sulfur or fermate. Discard plants at end of flowering season.

PROPAGATION:

Sow seeds in July for October to January bloom; keep seedlings as cool as possible, probably in large pots, tubs, or boxes outdoors until the first cool days of fall when they may be transferred to the greenhouse. Sow seeds in October for blooms beginning in February, and continuing until summer. A sowing in January will come into bloom by May.

Calla-Lily (*Zantedeschia* species)

White, fragrant flowers from January to June. Yellow or pink flowers from May to September.

CULTURE:

Nighttime temperature 60-65 degrees. Soil: equal parts garden loam, peat moss, and sand. Water freely and feed biweekly while in active growth; keep nearly dry and withhold fertilizer during period of semidormancy. Plant the white calla in August or September; yellow or pink callas January to April; one to a 6-inch pot, three to a 10-inch container. Provide sunny, warm, humid atmosphere. It is important that they be dried off annually following the flowering season. Rest for at least two or three months, then repot and start into new growth.

PROPAGATION:

Divide large clumps at repotting time. Seeds of the new Sunrise hybrids yield interesting new colors for callas; sow February to May at 65-75 degrees in moist potting soil.

Camellia

Pink, red, or white flowers from October to April. Select varieties of *C. japonica* that give early, midseason, and late bloom; two or three from each classification will give a constant succession of bloom over a long period. Outstanding varieties are available at reasonable prices by mail (see Appendix).

CULTURE:

Nighttime temperature 45-65 degrees. (Camellias are usually recommended only for cool greenhouses, but a grower in Ohio reports November to February bloom with a nighttime range of 55-65 degrees, and a greenhouse gardener in Mississippi reports September to April bloom in a range of 55-60 degrees.) Soil: equal parts garden loam, peat moss, and sand; the pH should be in a range of 4.0 to 5.5. Keep evenly moist. Provide sunny, airy, moist atmosphere in winter. Dampen floor of greenhouse every morning in winter. From March until August feed biweekly. Repot about every three years in March, April, or May. Place camellias outdoors in partially shaded, protected place in May or June and leave there until the first cool days of autumn. If you have time, disbud your camellias. (When the flower buds are large enough to tell one from the other, remove all buds in each cluster except the main or tip one.) This is done to gain larger, more perfect individual flowers at the expense of a greater quantity of less perfect ones.

PROPAGATION:

Make tip cuttings of half-ripened wood in August; insert in moist peat moss and sand; provide shade and high humidity. Sow seeds in similar conditions in March, April, or May; first blooms will not occur for three or four years.

Campanula

C. isophylla gives a cascade of blue, mauve, or white flowers intermittently from May to October. An ideal plant for shelf or basket culture.

CULTURE:

Nighttime temperature 45-55 degrees. Soil: equal parts garden loam, sand, peat moss, and leaf mold. Keep evenly moist, except on the dry side November to February. Provide bright light in summer, but protect from direct, hot sun. Trim back to shape after flowering.

PROPAGATION:

Make cuttings in January or February; insert in moist vermiculite; provide warmth (65-75 degrees), high humidity, and shade while roots are forming.

Candytuft

Pink or white flowers in April, May, and June.

CULTURE:

Nighttime temperature 50-65 degrees. Soil: equal parts garden loam, sand, and peat moss. Keep on the dry side, but do not allow to wilt. Discard at end of flowering season.

PROPAGATION:

Sow seeds of this annual in December for April bloom; in January for excellent cutting material in May and June.

Capsicum

Scarlet ornamental peppers from October to March.

30 Capsicum or Christmas pepper is easy to grow from seeds and makes a colorful, long-lasting plant in a home greenhouse. Author

CULTURE:

Nighttime temperature 50-60 degrees. Soil: equal parts garden loam, sand, and peat moss. Keep evenly moist. Feed biweekly. A tender perennial frequently treated as an annual, although it is possible to carry the plants over from year to year simply by cutting off the fruit crop in March and repotting with new soil.

PROPAGATION:

Sow seeds in April or May in warmth. Transplant individual seedlings to 3- or 4-inch pots, or 4- to 6-inch size. Summer outdoors to gain the heaviest set of peppers, but bring inside well ahead of frost.

Carnation

Lavender, orange, pink, red, white or yellow flowers from September to May.

CULTURE:

Nighttime temperature 50-55 degrees. Soil: two parts garden loam to one part each of peat moss and sand. Feed

31   Carnations are not difficult to grow in a home greenhouse, especially dwarfs like 'Juliet' which recently won a bronze medal from All-America Selections. ALL-AMERICA SELECTIONS

32 *Long-stemmed florist carnations require a string and wood support like this to guide the graceful, wandlike stems.* AUTHOR

biweekly. Provide sunny, airy, moist atmosphere. Carnations may be grown directly in a bench, in deep pots, or flats. Because my greenhouse is too warm for carnations in summer, I grow them in three redwood boxes that can be moved outdoors in June to a protected place and returned to the greenhouse in September. At that time the plants are groomed, staked, and tied. I disbud occasionally, leaving only the main flower bud on each stem. Old plants that have bloomed are discarded in late spring, the space they have occupied taken by new plants started early from cuttings.

PROPAGATION:

Make cuttings of sturdy tip growth in December, January, or February. Insert in moist vermiculite. Provide high humidity and keep the rooting medium evenly moist. When the cuttings are well rooted, transplant to pots of soil.

Celosia

The dwarf feather celosias and the dwarf crested cockscomb types like 'Jewel Box' have presented a new opportunity to enjoy these long-lasting annual flowers in the home greenhouse. They come in various autumn hues of chartreuse, golden yellow, crimson, and scarlet.

CULTURE:

Nighttime temperature 60 degrees. Soil: two parts garden loam to one each of peat moss and sand. Keep evenly moist. Provide full sun and plenty of fresh air. Discard when the flowers begin to lose their initial radiance.

PROPAGATION:

Sow seeds in warmth (70-80 degrees) in January or February for bloom in May. Sow in March or April for August; in July for an October-to-December show.

Centaurea

Blue, pink, rose, or white bachelor's-button flowers from January to May.

CULTURE:

Nighttime temperature 45-50 degrees. Soil: two parts garden loam, to one part each of peat moss and sand. Keep evenly moist. Provide full sun, ample fresh air, and feed biweekly as soon as seedlings are growing actively. Discard plants after flowering. The variety 'Jubilee Gem' is recommended for pot culture.

PROPAGATION:

Sow seeds in August or September for January and February flowers; sow seeds in December and January for spring bloom.

Cestrum

White flowers with heavenly fragrance at night, in summer, and bright green leaves all year.

CULTURE:

Nighttime temperature 60-68 degrees. Soil: equal parts garden loam, sand, peat moss and leaf mold. Keep evenly moist. Prune back as necessary in fall or winter to keep a convenient size. This plant, often called night jessamine, is a dependable perennial that requires no specific attention. *Cestrum nocturnum* is the species I grow; a friend favors *C. parqui*.

PROPAGATION:

Make 3-inch tip cuttings from February to June; root in moist vermiculite; provide warmth, humidity and shade while roots are forming.

Chrysanthemum

Bronze, chartreuse, lavender, pink, red, white, or yellow flowers from late August to January. (Professional growers achieve year-round bloom through a complicated program of lighting and shading.)

33 The space inside a greenhouse does not necessarily have to be given entirely to traditional benches and narrow walkways. Here a garden bench has been added so that the gardener can relax for a moment and appreciate the autumn glory of chrysanthemums. Author

CULTURE AND PROPAGATION:

Nighttime temperature 45-60 degrees. Soil: two parts garden loam to one part each of peat moss and sand. Provide sunny, airy atmosphere. You can go two ways with chrysanthemums in a home greenhouse. The first is the quickest way for the person who has a hectic schedule. Purchase plants in full bloom at a local florist from time to time. Mums are inexpensive items these days. It means a lot to me to be able to purchase a plant grown to perfection by a professional grower. Then, in what little time I have, I can pursue other gardening projects. The other way is to grow your own chrysanthemums from cuttings. Start in the spring by purchasing a collection of named varieties with as wide a natural blooming season as possible (the chart below shows a four-month span, from August 25 to December 25. The next spring you make 3-inch cuttings of new growth and discard the old plants. Do this in April, May, or June. Instead of rooting individual cuttings in a flat, or in small pots, expedite the matter: Plant four or five in each 6-inch bulb pan, using a medium composed of two parts garden loam to one part each of sand and peat moss. Keep moist and cool until roots form. Then provide plenty of sun. Keep soil evenly moist; never let it dry out severely. Feed biweekly. Summer outdoors if possible, and spray every week or two to assure vigorous, clean foliage. Pinch and stake to encourage compact, sturdy growth. Bring plants into the greenhouse by early September. Groom carefully. Tie and disbud, leaving only the largest bud on each main stem. Chrysanthemums set buds when the days are short. Therefore, your best plans for a

34 Early staking, combined with pinching of tip growth, produces sturdy, compact, flower-covered chrysanthemums in the home greenhouse. AUTHOR

long season of bloom may run amiss if a street light shines in your greenhouse, or if you work in the greenhouse at night in late summer and autumn while the buds are being set.

After flowering, cut back to an inch or two above the pot; put under the bench and keep barely moist. Bring to sunny warmth and apply more water about a month before you want to take cuttings.

Schedule for Chrysanthemums

Bloom Time		Variety	Color
August	25	'Rhapsody'	pink
September	15	'Salmon Cushion'	salmon-pink
	15	'Ermine'	white
	20	'Bronze Queen'	copper-bronze
	25	'Cecelia'	purple
October	1	'Fred Yule'	orange-bronze
	1	'Golden West'	yellow
	5	'Autumn Blaze'	oxblood-red
	5	'Oriole'	yellow
	10	'Enlightenment'	white
	10	'Cinderella'	pink
	15	'Revelation'	white
	15	'Fanfare'	bronze
	25	'Crescendo'	yellow
	25	'Warrior'	copper
November	1	'Welcome'	yellow
	1	'Cotton Queen'	white
	5	'Joan Berger'	orchid-pink
	5	'Temptation'	mauve-pink
	10	'Estrellita'	bronze
	15	'Dorothy Turner'	yellow & bronze
	20	'Sunnyside'	yellow
	20	'Magic Dot'	rose
Thanksgiving			'High Brow' (white), 'Ranger' (orange), 'Rubaiyat' (red), 'Thelma' (orange-scarlet), 'Thanksgiving White' and 'Thanksgiving Yellow.'
Christmas			'Christmas Red Improved,' and Elsie Kramer varieties in bronze, burgundy, pink, peach, rose, white, and yellow.

*35 Vivid, two-colored daisy flowers of cinerarias are the stars
of this home greenhouse in spring, along with single and double
petunias, geraniums, and fragrant flowering tobacco (nicotiana).
Shading is provided by Lumite Saran cloth.* AUTHOR

Cineraria

Blue, pink, purple, red, or white daisy flowers from January to May.

CULTURE AND PROPAGATION:

Nighttime temperature 45-55 degrees. Sow seeds in April,
May, or June for blooms in early winter; or after the weather
cools in August, September, or early October for March,
April, and May. Blooms occur generally about four weeks
after the plants become potbound. Transplant seedlings when
large enough to handle to 2¼-inch pots filled with equal parts
garden loam, peat moss, and sand. Group the pots together
so that they will always be moist. When roots begin to show
through the drainage holes, transplant directly to 5-inch clay
or plastic pots. Feed biweekly. Summer outdoors in a partially shaded position, as cool as possible. Move to green-

house before danger of frost in autumn. For extra-large specimen plants, transplant to 7- or 8-inch containers in January. Spray as necessary to control aphids. Discard plants at end of flowering season.

Cineraria is known botanically as *Senecio cruentus*. The *nana multiflora* strains grow about 15 inches tall, the *grandiflora* hybrids to 2 feet. All make superb plants; a dozen well grown ones will transform a small greenhouse into a spectacular flower show that will last for two or three months in a cool, moist, sunny atmosphere.

36   Dwarf citrus like the calamondin provide a year-round display of waxy, dark green foliage, fragrant flowers, and fruit in various stages of development. AUTHOR

Citrus

Fragrant white flowers intermittently all year followed by a long-lasting crop of fruit that may be chartreuse, yellow, or orange. Glossy, dark green foliage is attractive at all times.

CULTURE:

Nighttime temperature 50-68 degrees. Soil: two parts acid peat moss to one each of garden loam and sand. Keep evenly moist. Feed biweekly except November, December, and January. Provide full sun in fall, winter, and spring. Some shade in summer is all right although they can tolerate full, baking sun provided the soil is moist. Two lemons suitable for container gardening are *Citrus limonia ponderosa* and *C. l. meyeri*. Other kinds of citrus you will enjoy include Otaheite orange (*C. taitensis*), dwarf tangerine (*C. nobilis deliciosa*), Persian lime (*C. aurantifolia*), and calamondin (*C. mitis*).

PROPAGATION:

Tip cuttings of half-ripened wood may be rooted in moist, sandy soil in May, June, or July; provide shade and high humidity until new plants are established.

Clarkia

Orange, pink, red, salmon, or white flowers on long stems suitable for cutting.

CULTURE:

Nighttime temperature 50 degrees. Soil: equal parts garden loam, peat moss, and sand. Keep on dry side in full sun and provide ample fresh air. Artificial lighting in December and January will bring earlier bloom (see how-to under "Aster, China").

PROPAGATION:

Sow seeds of this annual in November for March, April, and May bloom; in January for April, May, and June. Space plants 5 or 6 inches apart in seedflats 4 inches deep.

Clematis

Pink, crimson, white, blue, or purple flowers from January to May.

37　*Clematis hybrids like this one are among the best of flowering vines for the home greenhouse.* J. HORACE MCFARLAND COMPANY

CULTURE:

Nighttime temperature 50-60 degrees. Soil: equal parts garden loam, peat moss, and sand. Add 1 tablespoon of lime to each 5- or 6-inch pot. Start by purchasing clematis plants in autumn from a commercial grower. Pot and place under bench in coolness until growth begins. Then bring to sunlight. Keep evenly moist and feed biweekly after growth begins. Provide 3-foot stake or trellis on which to climb. Clematis makes a spectacular showing in the greenhouse. Container plants may be summered outdoors in a place where the roots can be kept cool while the top of the plant receives sun. Allow to freeze in autumn, then trim back as necessary and bring to the greenhouse to begin another forcing period.

The varieties 'Barbara Dibley,' 'Barbara Jackman,' 'Comtesse de Bouchard,' 'Crimson Star,' 'Elsa Spath,' 'Henryi,' 'Lawsoniana,' 'Nelly Moser,' and 'Ramona' are suggested.

PROPAGATION:

Take 6-inch cuttings of half-ripened wood in June or July and insert in moist vermiculite; provide shade and high humidity while roots are forming.

Clerodendrum

Crimson, pink, or white flowers from March to November. *Clerodendrum fragrans pleniflorum* has large, coarse leaves that give off an unpleasant odor when disturbed, but each branch terminates in a cluster of pale pink, double blossoms set in reddish calyxes that yield the fragrance of "Cashmere Bouquet," a common name for the plant. Especially nice for a greenhouse used in the summer. *C. thomsonae*, the bleeding-heart vine, has clusters of pendant dark crimson flowers and attractive, inflated white calyxes. This species is a shrubby vine that can be kept to almost any convenient size. It blooms naturally in spring and makes a delightful addition to the greenhouse when trained up a trellis to the roof.

CULTURE:

Nighttime temperature 60-65 degrees. Soil: equal parts garden loam, peat moss, sand, and leaf mold. Water freely spring, summer, and fall; less in winter. Feed biweekly all year except October, November, December, and January. Prune back to convenient size, and repot in January. Provide shade in summer.

PROPAGATION:

Take 6-inch cuttings of half-ripened wood in January, February, or March; insert in moist vermiculite; provide warmth (70-80 degrees), shade, and high humidity until roots form.

Clivia

Apricot, salmon, scarlet, or yellow flowers in clusters at the top of a stiff stalk that rises from a fan of evergreen, strap-shaped leaves, March to June. A dependable amaryllid worthy of a place in almost every greenhouse. The stiff, lance-shaped leaves are always an attractive foil for flowering plants, and when in bloom the plants are truly handsome.

CULTURE:

Nighttime temperature 50-68 degrees. Soil: equal parts garden loam, sand, and peat moss. Keep evenly moist, except slightly less from October to January. Feed biweekly except during this period of semidormancy. Start by obtaining as large a plant as you can afford, and transplant it onto a larger container only when the present one is filled with roots. Do not ever dry off clivia, or cut away the foliage, as you may with amaryllis. A period of coolness (50 degrees nighttime temperature) in winter helps assure the flower crop.

PROPAGATION:

Sow seeds in spring; keep warm (75 degrees) and moist. First blooms may not occur for six or seven years. Large, multiple-crowned plants may be divided in January, February, or March.

Coleus

Rich foliage coloring all year as bright as many flowers.

CULTURE:

Nighttime temperature 50-68 degrees. Soil: equal parts garden loam, sand, and peat moss. Keep evenly moist. Provide full sun in fall, winter, and spring; partial shade in summer. Pinch back frequently, removing flower buds so that strength will be concentrated in production of large, colorful leaves. Watch constantly for mealybug. You may be able to control this insect by hand picking; otherwise spray according to container directions with aerosol of houseplant pesticide.

PROPAGATION:

Make cuttings in July or August from plants outdoors to have nice plants for winter and spring in the greenhouse. Sow seeds in May, June, July or August for vigorous young plants the following fall, winter, and spring. Seeds sown in February will germinate readily in moist vermiculite at 75 to 80 degrees.

Columnea

Orange, red, scarlet, or yellow flowers all year. Outstanding shelf and basket plants. *C. arguta* has 2-inch orange-red flowers with a yellow throat from September to November. 'Cayugan' bears reddish orange flowers from December to March on a spreading, more or less upright plant. 'Cornellian' has dark orange-yellow flowers with vivid yellow throat almost continuously. *C. hirta,* a trailer, has orange-scarlet flowers from March to May, and sometimes again in autumn. 'Red Arrow' is covered by vivid red flowers in winter and spring. 'Stavanger' covers pendant stems with 4-inch scarlet flowers over a period of several weeks, between March and June. *C. tulae* 'Flava' is an upright, Puerto Rican columnea with yellow flowers and everblooming habit. 'Yellow Dragon,' also everblooming, bears one to three flowers at each leaf axil, bright yellow with some red striping.

CULTURE:

Nighttime temperature 60-70 degrees. Soil: unmilled sphagnum moss combined with weekly feedings of very diluted houseplant fertilizer; or, equal parts garden loam, peat moss, leaf mold, and sand. Keep evenly moist. Provide partial sun from November through January, bright open shade balance of year. Columneas need a warm, humid atmosphere.

PROPAGATION:

Make 3-inch tip cuttings from March to May; root in moist vermiculite in warmth (75-85 degrees), high humidity, and shade.

Crassula

Pink, purple, or red flowers from May to November. *C. justicorderoyi* has dark leaves and dark pink flowers. 'Morgan's Pink' has clusters of bright pink flowers and gray leaves. 'Royal Purple' bears an abundance of purple flowers in August and September. *C. schmidti* practically covers itself from July until October with carmine-red flowers. *C. triebneri,* called "pink St. Andrew's cross," has chartreuse leaves, dotted with dark green, and pink flowers in summer. Light shade in summer will bring out the leaf markings. All of these crassulas are small-growing and choice plants for a shelf close to the glass.

CULTURE:

Nighttime temperature 55-68 degrees. Soil: two parts sand to one part each of peat moss and garden loam. Allow to dry out occasionally between waterings. Feed biweekly around the year, except November, December, and January. As crassulas mature, they form dense growth that may harbor mealybugs unless you inspect the plants frequently and spray when necessary.

PROPAGATION:

Leaf or stem cuttings root readily in moist potting soil and warmth at any season.

Crocus

Blue, lilac, purple, white, or yellow flowers in January, February, or March.

CULTURE:

Nighttime temperature 45-55 degrees. Soil equal parts garden loam, peat moss, and sand. Pot six corms to each 6-inch bulb pan in September, October, or November. Place in cool (about 45 degrees), dark place, and keep soil nicely moist while roots are forming. Forcing in a warm, sunny place can usually begin any time after eight weeks in coolness. For a succession of bloom, start forcing at ten- to fourteen-day intervals from December until March. After flowering, put the pots under the bench—or wherever you have space for them; keep the soil moist, and when the ground outdoors is workable, plant them in a permanent place. Do not try to force the same bulbs again.

Crossandra

Spikes of salmon-orange flowers, everblooming above glossy, dark green leaves.

CULTURE:

Nighttime temperature 55-68 degrees. Soil: two parts peat moss or leaf mold to one part each garden loam and sand. Keep evenly moist and feed biweekly. Abundant sun in winter will promote heavy flowering, but shade is needed in summer.

PROPAGATION:

Three-inch tip cuttings root easily in moist potting soil, warmth, and high humidity at any time. This plant is delightful in terra-cotta pots or white plastic, and nice to propagate as a gift for your friends since it is excellent for house culture.

Croton (*Codiaeum* species)

Brown, chartreuse, pink, red, and yellow foliage. Alberts & Merkel Brothers (Appendix) list many named varieties. It is possible to select almost any leaf coloring that will blend or contrast pleasingly with flowering plants in the greenhouse.

CULTURE:

Nighttime temperature 60-75 degrees. Soil: equal parts garden loam, sand, peat moss, and leaf mold. Keep evenly moist and feed biweekly. Crotons need warmth and high humidity, but sufficient air circulation to discourage red-spider mite.

Provide sun in winter, but some shade from May to September.

PROPAGATION:

Six-inch tip cuttings may be rooted from February to June in high humidity and warmth (70-80 degrees).

Cyclamen

Crimson, pink, red, violet, or white flowers from November to April.

CULTURE:

Nighttime temperature 50-65 degrees. Soil: equal parts garden loam, peat moss, and sand. Cyclamen grows from a fleshy tuber similar to that of the gloxinia and tuberous-rooted begonia. The quickest way to acquire a blooming cyclamen plant for your greenhouse is to buy one heavily budded at a local florist in November, December, or January. In your greenhouse, provide a cool, moist atmosphere, and protection from direct sun at midday. Keep the soil moist at all times and feed biweekly. The plant will bloom heavily for several months. When flowering ceases, withhold water until the leaves have died down. Keep nearly dry, with the pot on its side under the bench, until July. Repot then, and start into growth in a cool, shaded place.

PROPAGATION:

Sow seeds in June, July, or August for bloom approximately 18 months later. Start in a mixture of equal parts peat moss and sand. Keep warm and moist.

Cyrtanthus

Orange, pink, white, or yellow flowers, borne in clusters atop graceful stems in November, December, and January. This small amaryllid sends up an abundance of narrow, strap-shaped leaves, and flowers freely at a time when blooms are much appreciated.

38   Cyclamen, which grows from a tuber, gives a beautiful display of flowers and variegated foliage most of the winter and spring in a sunny, airy, moist greenhouse. GEORGE W. PARK SEED COMPANY

CULTURE:

Nighttime temperature 50-65 degrees. Soil: equal parts garden loam, peat moss, and sand. Obtain bulbs from August to October and plant on arrival, about six in a 6-inch pot. Keep under the bench in coolness (about 50-60 degrees at night) until top growth shows. Then bring to a sunny, warm position in the greenhouse. When the blossoms have withered, cut back the bloom stems. Continue watering and feeding as for other plants in active growth. My cyrtanthus are placed outdoors along with amaryllis for the summer, fed biweekly, but generally neglected. In September, before frost threatens, water is

withheld and the plants are brought into the greenhouse, the
pots turned on their sides beneath the benches. After about
eight weeks of resting they are repotted, and all the old leaves
cut back to the top of the pot. In a warm, sunny position, with
the soil kept evenly moist, new growth begins immediately,
and flowering occurs within a few weeks. However, repotting
is not necessary every year; if you don't have time, simply cut
back the foliage after resting, and place plants on bench in
warmth.

PROPAGATION:

Divide old plants at repotting time in October or November.

Didiscus

Lavender-blue flowers from November to May. The blue
lace flower.

CULTURE:

Nighttime temperature 45-55 degrees. Soil: two parts garden loam to one part each of peat moss and sand. Keep evenly
moist and feed biweekly.

PROPAGATION:

Sow seeds of this annual in June or July for bloom December to February; sow in August or September for flowers from
February to May; sow in January for blooms beginning in
April. Grow didiscus plants close together in a 4- or 5-inch-
deep flat. Discard at end of flowering season.

Dimorphotheca

Apricot, orange, white, or yellow flowers from March to
June. Called African daisy.

CULTURE:

Nighttime temperature 50-65 degrees. Soil: two parts garden loam to one each of peat moss and sand. Keep evenly
moist and feed biweekly. Provide full, baking sun in winter,
as on a shelf close to the glass. Grow in low pots or a seedflat.

This annual yields a bountiful flower crop in a sunny, warm, airy atmosphere; the blossoms close at dusk.

PROPAGATION:

Sow seeds in July or August for bloom the following late winter and spring.

Dipladenia

Rosy pink, funnel-shaped flowers from June to December on twining stems set with leathery, dark green leaves. Formerly called *Mandevilla*.

CULTURE:

Nighttime temperature 55-65 degrees. Soil: equal parts garden loam, peat moss, sand, and leaf mold, with the addition of one part chipped charcoal. Keep evenly moist and feed biweekly, except during semidormancy from December to February; then keep on dry side and withhold fertilizer. Train this vine on a small trellis inserted into the pot. Dipladenia does well in a 10- to 12-inch pot or tub. Repot every two or three years. Provide abundant sun in winter and spring, but partial shade in summer and early fall. A very choice plant that deserves to be better known. In return for almost no attention it gives a long blooming season. Check leaf undersides frequently in order to detect signs of mealybug, a potentially serious foe.

PROPAGATION:

Three-inch cuttings of vigorous sideshoots will root in February, March, or April; keep warm (70-80 degrees), moist, and shaded until roots form.

Echeveria

Coral, crimson, orange-red, or yellow flowers from December to April. *E. derenbergi* has orange-red flowers on short stems from February to April above pale green leaves edged red. *E. elegans* has coral-pink flowers and blue-green leaves. *E. pulvinata* or chenille plant, has velvety, blue-green leaves

39 When the base of a single leaf of echeveria is inserted in moist potting soil it roots and soon sends up a new plant, as shown here. AUTHOR

edged with crimson, and crimson and yellow bell flowers in January and February. It needs sun and coolness for best foliage coloration. *E. retusa* has blue-green leaves and coral-red flowers from December to February. Echeverias require almost no attention, yet they give interest all year; excellent shelf plants.

CULTURE:

Nighttime temperature 55-68 degrees. Soil: two parts sand to one part each of peat moss and garden loam. Provide full sun, except a little shade is beneficial in midsummer. Feed biweekly. Keep evenly moist, generally, but allow to dry out occasionally.

PROPAGATION:

Insert cuttings in moist sand from March to June for vigorous young plants the following winter and spring.

Episcia

Blue, lilac, red, scarlet, white, or yellow flowers, especially from March to August, but nearly everblooming in a warm, bright, humid atmosphere. The foliage may be green, all the way from a light lettuce color to a dark shade; or bronze to copper, or a silvery to purplish hue; sometimes the leaves are variegated with creamy white or soft pink. The foliage of some varieties is hairy and that of others is smooth or glossy.

CULTURE:

Nighttime temperature 60-75 degrees. Soil: equal parts garden loam, sand, peat moss, and leaf mold; or, grow in plain unmilled sphagnum moss. Feed biweekly. Episcias are tolerant of various light conditions; with moist soil and a humid atmosphere, they will do well in full winter sun. At other seasons, some shading is desirable. Episcias are cultivated primarily for rich, textured, colorful foliage, but in the right conditions they are excellent flowering plants. Episcias are among the most beautiful of all hanging basket plants. Enjoy them in a flowerpot hung up with a wire or string, or fill a wire or redwood basket with rooted cuttings. Soon you will have a cascade of luxuriant foliage.

PROPAGATION:

Remove stolons and insert the stems in a moist vermiculite or sphagnum moss. Rooting will occur within a few days in warmth and high humidity. The most vigorous episcias are those that are young; therefore, it is a good idea to start new stolons every year or so, discarding the old plants, or cutting them back severely after the new crop of cuttings is well on its way.

40 *Eucharis is one of the best of all medium-size foliage plants, but when it blooms, it is a glorious exotic. It is easy to grow in almost any home greenhouse.* AUTHOR

Eucharis

White, daffodil-like flowers appear on graceful but sturdy stems as often as four times a year; these stand slightly above the dark green leaves which grow about 18 to 24 inches tall and resemble those of spathiphyllum. Even without the exquisite flowers, eucharis is an outstanding, durable foliage plant, much less prone to tip dieback than most.

CULTURE:

Nighttime temperature 55-70 degrees. Soil: equal parts garden loam, peat moss, and sand. Pot one dormant eucharis bulb
in a 6-inch pot whenever received from grower. Keep evenly
moist. Provide sunny, moist, airy atmosphere. Feed biweekly.
Flowers are not likely to appear until the original bulb has
multiplied and practically filled the pot with roots. If flowers
do not appear of their own accord at this point, water less, allowing the soil to approach dryness before adding a little
moisture; this treatment usually induces flowering and can be
repeated three or four times yearly.

PROPAGATION:

Divide old, crowded clumps in any season, but remember,
eucharis flowers best when potbound.

Euphorbia

Euphorbia mili and its varieties, all forms of the popular
crown of thorns, bear lemon-yellow, pink, or scarlet flowers
almost all year. (See "Poinsettia" for a discussion of *Euphorbia pulcherrima.*)

CULTURE:

Nighttime temperature 55-68 degrees. Soil: two parts sand
to one each of peat moss and garden loam. Water freely, then
allow to dry out. Feed about once a month. Provide full sun
from October to April, some shade the balance of the year.

PROPAGATION:

Make cuttings any time from March to July, first letting the
cut portions dry in open air before inserting in moist sand.

Exacum

Lavender-blue, star-shaped flowers, accented by golden an-
thers, from December to May. Lightly fragrant.

CULTURE:

Nighttime temperature 50-65 degrees. Soil: equal parts garden loam, peat moss, and sand. Keep evenly moist. Feed biweekly from time buds show until flowering season is well advanced.

PROPAGATION:

Sow seeds in May or June for blooms the following winter and spring. Discard at end of one season.

Felicia

Blue daisy flowers from December to May. Sometimes called Agathea.

CULTURE:

Nighttime temperature 50-60 degrees (never lower than 45). Soil: equal parts garden loam, peat moss, and sand. Keep evenly moist. Feed biweekly while in active growth. Water occasionally with acidifying solution made by mixing 1 teaspoon nitrate of soda to 1 gallon of water.

PROPAGATION:

Sow seeds any time from January to July for bloom the following winter and spring. Pinch seedlings several times to encourage compact, bushy growth. Cuttings from established plants root easily in moist vermiculite in May or June.

Freesia

Orange, pink, white, or yellow flowers with heavenly fragrance from December to March.

CULTURE:

Nighttime temperature 50 degrees. Soil: equal parts garden loam, peat moss, and sand. Plant six corms to each 6-inch pot; make your first planting in August and continue every two or three weeks until late November or December. Keep cool for

41 Freesias grow from fall-planted corms and thrive in a home greenhouse that is sunny, airy, cool, and moist in the winter. Here grower James McNair has brought a pot of the deliciously scented flowers inside to enjoy in his townhouse. AUTHOR

about six weeks, then bring the first pot up to the bench to begin forcing. Repeat this procedure about every two weeks. Corms planted in August will yield January bloom, September for February, October for March, and December for April. Keep evenly moist while in active growth and feed biweekly. After flowering ceases, dry off, and keep dormant until planting time.

PROPAGATION:

Seeds of hybrid strains planted in February or March will give bloom the following December and January. Plant in a wooden flat 6 or 7 inches deep. Summer outdoors, and do not allow to dry out. Avoid transplanting. The key to first-year blooms from seeds is keeping seedlings in constant growth with no setbacks.

Fuchsia

Pink, purple, red, rose, or white pendant flowers from April to September. Choose from varieties suited to pots, baskets, or

42   Fuchsias may be difficult houseplants, but they are among the best performers among flowering greenhouse specimens, especially the everblooming 'Gartenmeister Bohnstedt' (shown). AUTHOR

training as standards. The old-fashioned honeysuckle fuchsia
(*F. triphylla* 'Gartenmeister Bohnstedt') with its orange-red
bells is nearly everblooming in my greenhouse.

CULTURE:

Nighttime temperature 55-60 degrees. Soil: equal parts garden loam, peat moss, and sand. Keep evenly moist. Feed biweekly while plants are in active growth and flowering heavily.
A feeding of fish emulsion fertilizer every week or two will
give excellent results. Prune and repot in the spring. Fuchsias
need sun in fall and winter, some shade in spring and summer.

PROPAGATION:

Root cuttings in July, August, or September in order to have
vigorous young plants for the following spring and summer.
These will be ready for 5- or 6-inch pots in March.

Gardenia

Fragrant, creamy white flowers in winter and spring.

CULTURE:

Nighttime temperature 62-65 degrees. Soil: equal parts garden loam, peat moss, and sand, with a pH of 5.0 to 5.5. Keep
evenly moist. While in active growth, feed biweekly. Soil on
the alkaline side will cause yellowing leaves; correct by applying a solution made by mixing 1 ounce iron sulfate in 2
gallons of water; repeat every three or four weeks until the
foliage resumes dark green coloration. Provide sun in fall and
winter, partial shade in spring and summer. Transplant in
April, May, or June, moving to one size larger pot when the
previous one has been filled with roots. Summer outdoors as
for azaleas.

PROPAGATION:

Three-inch cuttings of sturdy young side shoots may be
rooted from January to April; provide warmth (70-80 degrees), high humidity, and a moist rooting medium (vermiculite or equal parts peat moss and sand will do nicely).

Gazania

Orange, red, white, or yellow daisy flowers from January to October. These close at night, but on a sunny day they make a vivid picture. The gray-green leaves grow in low rosettes. Each leaf turns over at night to reveal a white, woolly underside.

CULTURE:

Nighttime temperature 50-60 degrees. Soil: equal parts garden loam, peat moss, and sand. A tender perennial which may be kept year after year in a cool, sunny, airy greenhouse. Trim out old growth in late spring and again in September or October. Repot annually in spring. Keep on dry side to induce semidormancy in autumn.

PROPAGATION:

Sow seeds in May or June for bloom beginning the following January.

43 Geraniums, like begonias, have such diversity that an entire greenhouse may be filled with them for flowers every day of the year, not to mention scented foliage and tricolored leaves like these of 'Mrs. Cox' which are green, brown, orange, and cream.
AUTHOR

Geranium (*Pelargonium* species)

It is possible to have flowers all the time and in all colors from geraniums. Besides, they offer colorful foliage and fragrance. Every flowering greenhouse should have at least a dozen named varieties of *Pelargonium hortorum,* the common geranium, and at least three or four scenteds. If you like geraniums, collect colors and kinds that appeal most. Based on flowering qualities, length of bloom season, and all-around performance, I recommend these geraniums for a flowering greenhouse:

Hortorum	*Fancyleaf*	*Domesticum*
'Always'	'Carlton's Velma'	'African Belle'
'Cuba'	'Dark Beauty'	'Bimbo'
'Dawn'	'Flowers of Spring'	'Chicago Market'
'Fiat'	'Mrs. Henry Cox'	'Easter Greetings'
'Gallant'	'Verona'	'Grand Slam'
'Gertrude'		'Mme. Layal'
'Gleam'		'Waltztime'
'Merry Gardens White'		
'Patricia Audette'		
'Paul Crampel Improved'		
'Red Perfection'		
'Wicked Lady'		

Peltatum	*Scented*	*Odd and Rare*
'Charles Turner'	'Apricot'	'Carmel'
'Diener's Lavender'	'Clorinda'	'Jeanne'
'Galilee'	'Coconut'	'Oliver Kuser'
'Joseph Warren'	'Fair Ellen'	'Red Rosebud'
'L'Elegante'	'Joy Lucille'	*rutaceum*
'Mrs. Banks'	'Mrs. Kingsley'	'Souvenir de Mirande'
'Victorville'	'Old Spice'	
	'Prince of Orange'	
	'Prince Rupert Variegated'	
	'Red-flowered Rose'	
	'Rober's Lemon Rose'	
	'Scarlet Unique'	

CULTURE:

Nighttime temperature 50-60 degrees. Soil: equal parts garden loam, peat moss, and sand. Keep evenly moist. Feed biweekly from January to September with fertilizer low in nitrogen content. Provide sunny, airy atmosphere. All geraniums benefit from a summer outdoors. The regals or Lady Washingtons (*P. domesticum* types) need to be cut back severely after flowering, usually about May or June, repotted and kept outdoors in summer in abundant sun so that flower buds will be set for the following year.

Regular geraniums that have been outdoors all summer may be too large to move back into the greenhouse in autumn. Meet this problem by making cuttings of all the kinds you want in August or September, leaving old plants to Jack Frost; or you can cut back old plants in autumn, repot, and keep on the dry side until January. Then provide more water and begin to feed biweekly; in warmth and sun the plants will be in full bloom by the middle of February.

PROPAGATION:

Make cuttings from March to August for vigorous, young, flowering plants the following fall, winter, and spring. Geranium cuttings may be rooted directly in 5-inch pots of regular potting soil; this avoids transplanting shock, and saves time. Keep cuttings on dry side the first ten to fourteen days, then evenly moist. Best rooting occurs in 60-degree nighttime temperatures. To achieve compact, well-branched geraniums, pinch back the tips two or three times after newly rooted cuttings are in active growth. The regals are best propagated from cuttings of non-flowering shoots in July; these are kept growing without check, and transplanted as required by the roots to a 6- or 7-inch pot by January.

Gerbera

Cream, orange, pink, red, or salmon flowers, 3 to 5 inches across, single or double, and borne on long, wiry stems, from December to May.

44 *Gerbera, the daisy from South Africa, makes a superb all-season flowering plant in a home greenhouse. Start from seeds, or purchase established plants.* BODGER SEEDS, LTD.

CULTURE:

Nighttime temperature 50-60 degrees. Soil: equal parts garden loam, peat moss, and sand; add 2 teaspoons of lime to each 10-inch pot of soil mixture. Keep evenly moist. Set three plants to a standard 10-inch pot. Provide sunny, moist, airy atmosphere. Feed biweekly. Summer outdoors as container plants.

PROPAGATION:

Divide old, crowded clumps in June. Sow seeds in January or February at 55-60 degrees for bloom the following winter and spring. Plant fresh seeds with the sharp end down.

Gladiolus

Gladiolus tristis and *G. blandus* provide graceful spikes of pink, red, or white evening-scented flowers in February, March, and April.

CULTURE:

Nighttime temperature 50-60 degrees. Soil: equal parts garden loam, peat moss, and sand. Pot corms in October, 2 inches deep. After flowering, ripen off and store dry for the summer as freesias. Ordinary gladiolus, especially those of the miniature varieties, are also useful in a small, sunny greenhouse; plant corms in a deep bench in January or early February for blooms in April or May.

PROPAGATION:

Corms increase naturally every year.

Gloriosa

Scarlet and yellow flowers from March to May.

CULTURE:

Nighttime temperature 60-68 degrees. Soil: equal parts garden loam, peat moss, sand, and leaf mold. Plant one tuber to a standard 6-inch pot or bulb pan, or three to an 8- to 10-inch container. Keep barely moist until growth begins, then keep evenly moist, and feed biweekly until flowering is well along. Provide a small trellis on which to train the clambering stems. After blooming, keep in active growth until June or July, then dry off and rest until autumn.

PROPAGATION:

Sow seeds in February or March; plant ¼-inch deep in moist peat moss and sand; keep warm (70-80 degrees). Offsets may be removed from large tubers at repotting time in autumn.

45 . *Gloxinias like this one grow easily from seeds or tubers, with first flowers opening in approximately four months and continuing for several weeks.* HORT-PIX

Gloxinia

Velvety single or double flowers in all colors except bright yellow from January to September.

CULTURE:

Nighttime temperature 62-68 degrees. Soil: equal parts garden loam, peat moss, sand, and leaf mold. Keep evenly moist and feed biweekly while plants are in active growth. Do not apply icy cold water at any time. Plant tubers in February, March, or April in 5- or 6-inch pots for summer bloom. Plant tubers, or buy young started plants, in August, September, or October for winter bloom. A home greenhouse owner in Louisiana reports gloxinias in full bloom from December to March by providing supplemental fluorescent light from six to eight-thirty A.M. from November until spring.

PROPAGATION:

Sow seeds at 70 to 75 degrees in January or February for June to September flowers. Sow seeds in September or October in warm, humid place, for outstanding blooms the following March, April, and May. Leaf cutting with a 1-inch leaf-stalk will root quickly in moist vermiculite; after roots form at the base of the leaf-stalk, a tuber begins to grow, its size depending on how long the leaf can be kept in good condition. Eventually it will die down, and a gloxinia plant will sprout from the newly formed tuber.

Godetia

Lavender, pink, red, or white flowers from April to June.

CULTURE:

Nighttime temperature 50-55 degrees. Soil: two parts sand to one part each of garden loam, and peat moss. Grow on the dry side. Provide full sun. Discard at end of the flowering season.

PROPAGATION:

Sow seeds from September to January and keep at 68 to 75 degrees until after germination. Plant in shallow pots or flats. Godetias do not thrive outdoors in summer in most parts of the United States owing to high nighttime temperatures, but they make an excellent greenhouse crop.

Gypsophila

Crimson, pink, or white baby's-breath flowers at almost any season, depending on when seeds are sown.

CULTURE:

Nighttime temperature 45-55 degrees. Soil: equal parts garden loam, peat moss, and sand. Keep evenly moist. Feed biweekly after seedlings are well-established. This quick-growing annual makes good filler material for background and in-between the more rigid forms and textures of other greenhouse plants. Frequent cutting will help keep the plants in good condition over a long period of time. Discard when they cease to be attractive.

PROPAGATION:

Sow seeds any time except October, November, and December. A deep seed flat or 8-inch standard flowerpots make good containers.

Haemanthus

Orange-scarlet, red, or white flowers from May to October, the time depending on the species cultivated. *H. albiflos* has interesting, small white flowers in September or October. *H. coccineus* has red flowers in the spring, followed by sturdy, attractive green foliage in summer. Dry it off in September and rest at about 50 degrees until March; then bring to top of bench to warmth and keep moist until flower buds appear. *H. katherinae* and *H. multiflorus* bloom from May to July, with practically evergreen foliage (it dies down in winter, followed immediately by new leaves).

CULTURE:

Nighttime temperature 50-60 degrees. Soil: equal parts garden loam, peat moss, and sand. Provide full sun in late winter and spring, some shade in summer. Feed biweekly from March to August. Keep on dry side in winter. Repot every three or four years.

PROPAGATION:

Remove offsets from large plants in the spring and pot separately.

Heliotrope

Blue, purple, or white fragrant flowers from November to May.

CULTURE:

Nighttime temperature 60 degrees. Soil: equal parts garden loam, peat moss, and sand. Keep evenly moist and feed biweekly. Heliotrope is a tender perennial frequently cultivated outdoors as an annual, but easily grown in a greenhouse as a basket plant, in a pot, or in tree form. Cut it back occasionally to encourage new growth. Provide sunny, airy, moist atmosphere.

PROPAGATION:

Sow seeds in May or June to have young flowering plants the following fall and winter. Make cuttings in July from plants growing outdoors.

Herbs

Chives, parsley, borage, mints (orange, pepper, and pineapple), basil, and lemon-verbena bring fragrance and some flower color to the greenhouse all year.

CULTURE:

Nighttime temperature 50-65 degrees. Soil: equal parts garden loam, peat moss, and sand. Keep evenly moist and feed every two or three weeks. Purchase small pot plants of chives at the supermarket, obtain by mail, or dig from garden. Chives will do better in a greenhouse if they are frozen for a short period in late fall outdoors, then brought inside and forced. Start with parsley by purchasing a young potted plant in autumn, or sow seeds any time. Borage grows easily from seeds sown July, August, or September for flowering plants the following February, March, April, and May. Transplant these to the outdoor garden, cut back, and they will bloom until fall. Dig some self-sown seedlings from the garden before frost, pot, and place in the greenhouse. Borage yields many starry lavender-blue flowers, especially nice on a shelf so that you can look up to see them. The mints grow easily in a large pot of moist soil; cut back occasionally to promote new growth and divide every year or two. Obtain plants from a mail-order supplier (see Appendix). Common sweet basil and the more ornamental 'Dark Opal' may be sown in July, August, or September to yield attractive plants the following winter and spring. Lemon-verbena is a tender perennial which may be obtained as a young plant from a mail-order supplier. It needs full sun and evenly moist soil (except slightly on the dry side in autumn for a rest period).

Hibiscus, Chinese

Carmine, red, rose, scarlet, white, or yellow flowers all year.

CULTURE:

Nighttime temperature 50-70 degrees. Soil: equal parts garden loam, peat moss, and sand. Keep evenly moist. Feed

46   Chinese hibiscus is a choice subject for the flowering green-house because it produces blooms on new growth and can, there-fore, be kept pruned to any convenient size. AUTHOR

biweekly. Prune back as necessary to keep a convenient size. Provide full sun from fall to spring. May be summered out-doors in a partially shaded place.

PROPAGATION:

Take 4-inch stem cuttings from March to July. Root in moist vermiculite; provide high humidity and some shade until roots have formed. Because *Hibiscus rosa-sinensis* hybrids bloom on new growth, it is not unusual to have the flamboyant flowers on cuttings still in the rooting medium.

Hoya

H. carnosa, the old-fashioned wax plant, bears pink and white flowers from March to August. The waxy, dark green leaves on twining stems are interesting all year. Other hoyas, more recently introduced, offer fascination for a collector of unusual plants.

CULTURE:

Nighttime temperature 55-65 degrees. Soil: equal parts garden loam, peat moss, leaf mold, and sand. Let dry out, then water freely. Provide small trellis on which to train the stems. Abundant sun from fall to spring helps promote heavy flowering, but some shade in summer is desirable.

PROPAGATION:

Cuttings made from March to June will root easily in moist vermiculite in a warm, humid place. Hoya may be layered simply by covering a portion of the stem, including a set of leaf nodes, with moist potting soil; after rooting occurs, sever from the main plant. When you take cuttings from hoya, remember to leave any stem or "spur" from which flowers have been borne; next year's flowers will come from the same place.

Hyacinth

Blue, pink, rose, white, or yellow fragrant blooms from December to March.

47 *Hyacinths with their heady aroma grow from bulbs planted in autumn and kept cool and moist in darkness for an eight-week rooting period, after which time they can be brought to the greenhouse for blooms a few weeks later.* PAUL GENEREUX

CULTURE:

Nighttime temperature 40-70 degrees, depending on forcing time desired. Soil: equal parts garden loam, peat moss, and sand. Keep evenly moist. Feeding is not necessary. Pot Roman hyacinth bulbs in September for December bloom.

Plant Dutch hyacinths from September to November for
bloom in January, February, or March. Keep at 40 to 50
degrees for a rooting period of about eight weeks. After
potting, I put my hyacinths on a shelf in my unheated garage.
The temperatures there are above freezing, but cool enough
to promote good root growth. The blooms push up rapidly
at 65 to 70 degrees, slower at 60, and sturdiest growth occurs
at 45 to 55 degrees. Plant hyacinths outdoors in a permanent
place in the garden after flowering. Do not force the same
bulbs again.

Hydrangea

Blue, pink, or white flowers from March to May.

CULTURE AND PROPAGATION:

Nighttime temperature 50-60 degrees. Soil: two parts
garden loam to one part each of leaf mold, peat moss, and
sand. Add two tablespoons of superphosphate to a peck of
the soil mixture. To start hydrangea, buy a plant just coming
into bloom at your local florist in spring. Make cuttings in
March or April from strong flowering shoots 4 to 5 inches
long. Root at 60 degrees. Transplant to 5-inch pots, and by
fall move the plants to 7- or 8-inch pots. In October, November, and December keep at about 45 degrees and on the dry
side. The leaves will fall, but this period of dormancy is
necessary. In January move to the top of the bench to about
50 degrees nighttime temperature where the atmosphere is
moist and sunny in the daytime, and keep the soil evenly
moist. Beginning in February, feed biweekly with a liquid
houseplant fertilizer. To produce blue flowers, water in one
teaspoon of aluminum sulfate to each 6-inch pot every two
weeks in January and February. Unless you have plenty of
time to keep hydrangeas on a careful schedule through the
year, simply discard the plant after it finishes flowering, and
buy a new one the following spring just as it is beginning to
come into bloom. Even one hydrangea makes a spectacular
showing in the home greenhouse.

Impatiens

Orange, orchid, pink, purple, red, rose, scarlet, salmon,
or white flowers all year.

48 *Impatiens, while somewhat temperamental in the average heated house or apartment, grow like weeds in an airy, moist home greenhouse. The Cyclone hybrids (shown), developed from species recently discovered in New Guinea, have beautifully variegated and colored foliage as well as large flowers.* AUTHOR

CULTURE:

Nighttime temperature 50-60 degrees. Soil: equal parts garden loam, peat moss, and sand. Keep evenly moist. Feed biweekly. Provide moist atmosphere with some fresh air and full sun in winter. Impatiens do well in shade at other seasons.

PROPAGATION:

Plant seeds in May, June, or July for bloom the following fall, winter, and spring. Cuttings made from plants outdoors in July and August will also give fall to spring bloom.

Iris, Dutch

Blue, white, or yellow flowers from January to April.

CULTURE:

Nighttime temperature 45-55 degrees. Plant corms in September and keep in a cool place outside until danger of frost, and then move inside to under the bench, and preferably where the temperature will be on the cool side (45-50 degrees) until November or December. Then begin forcing at 50-55 degrees, or slightly warmer for faster growth. *I. reticulata* is a dwarf-growing iris that may be planted three to a 5-inch pot and kept cool at all times. In the cool greenhouse it will flower in the spring with no special treatment, and make an excellent addition there. After flowering, move bulbous irises to a protected coldframe. They may be planted out to a permanent place in the garden after the weather is warm.

Ixia

Crimson, orange, pink, purple, white, or yellow flowers in February, March, or April. Sparaxis gives about the same color range and blooming season; provide the same culture as for ixia.

CULTURE:

Nighttime temperature 50-60 degrees. Pot five or six bulbs in September, October, or November to each 5-inch container. Keep cool (40-50 degrees) until about December so that the bulbs will form good root systems. Then move to the top of the bench to a sunny place and water freely after growth starts. January bloom is possible if bulbs are started into active growth in December. After flowering, treat as freesias.

PROPAGATION:

By offsets removed at repotting time in autumn.

Ixora

Pink, red, white, or yellow flowers intermittently all year. *I. acuminata* has white flowers in April and May. *I. chinensis* opens cinnabar-red flowers almost year 'round. 'McGee's Yellow' and 'Henry Morat' (pink) add interest to the color range.

CULTURE:

Nighttime temperature 55-65 degrees. Soil: two parts acid peat moss to one each of garden loam and sand. Keep evenly moist. Provide warmth and high humidity all year; full sun from fall to spring, partial shade in warm weather. A nice flowering-size ixora will do well in an 8-inch pot. Prune to shape in February or March.

PROPAGATION:

From March to May, cuttings of half-ripened wood with four pairs of leaves will root readily in moist vermiculite, at 70-75 degrees.

Jacobinia

Orange, red, rose, pink, or yellow flowers off and on all year.

CULTURE:

Nighttime temperature 55-65 degrees. Soil: equal parts garden loam, peat moss, and sand. Keep evenly moist. Feed biweekly. The best plants are those started from tip cuttings made immediately after flowering. These will form outstanding specimen plants within a year's time. They depend on a constant supply of moisture, lots of sun, and regular feedings to stay in good growth.

PROPAGATION:

Take 3-inch tip cuttings after a flowering period; root in moist vermiculite; provide warmth, high humidity and shade while roots are forming.

Jasminum

White or yellow fragrant flowers in autumn or winter.

CULTURE:

Nighttime temperature 45-55 degrees (*J. mesnyi,* syn. *J. primulinum,* and *J. officinale grandiflorum*), or 55-65 degrees (*J. gracillimum* and *J. sambac*). Soil: equal parts garden loam, peat moss, leaf mold, and sand. Keep evenly moist. Feed biweekly except from September to December. Provide full sun and airy, moist atmosphere. Prune in the spring after flowering.

PROPAGATION:

Make cuttings of vigorous, firm growth from March to September; root in moist vermiculite at 65-75 degrees; provide humidity and shade until roots form.

Kaempferia

Lavender or yellow flowers, lightly fragrant, from May to August. *K. decora* grows from 12 to 24 inches tall and bears a constant display of brilliant yellow, 3-inch flowers. *K. roscoeana,* to 6 inches, has iridescent foliage, as handsome as a peacock's feather, and small lavender flowers, similar to an African violet in shape, that open fresh nearly every day all summer.

CULTURE:

Nighttime temperature 60-70 degrees. Soil: equal parts garden loam, peat moss, leaf mold, and sand. Keep evenly moist in spring and summer; nearly dry in fall and winter. Do not subject dormant roots to temperature below 50 degrees. Grow in partial sun to shade, provide high humidity, and feed biweekly in spring and summer.

PROPAGATION:

Divide large, well-established rootstocks February, March, or April.

Kalanchoe

Orange, scarlet, or yellow flowers from January to May. The chief flowering kalanchoes are hybrids derived from *K. blossfeldiana. K. beharensis* is a starkly sculptured species with gray-green leaves heavily overlaid with reddish bronze hairs. *K. tubiflora* has pinkish brown stems and cylindrical leaves of blue-green spotted purple; tiny new plants form at leaf tips. There are other interesting kalanchoes that are useful in the greenhouse; they are unusual in flower, and the foliage adds year-round beauty.

CULTURE:

Nighttime temperature 50-70 degrees. Soil: equal parts garden loam, peat moss, and sand. Keep evenly moist, except allow to be on the dry side occasionally. Feed biweekly from February to August.

PROPAGATION:

Sow seeds of *K. blossfeldiana* types from January to July for blooms the following winter and spring. Flower buds are set during short days. Early sowing means that seedlings will be larger the following year; those started late may bloom while still in 2-inch pots. These kalanchoes, like all other species, are easily propagated from leaf and tip cuttings, but in my experience, the blossfeldianas propagated vegetatively bloom later than those grown from seeds.

Lachenalia

Red or yellow flowers in January, February, March, or April. The cape cowslip.

CULTURE:

Nighttime temperature 50 degrees. Soil: equal parts garden loam, peat moss, and sand. Plant six corms to 6-inch pot in August or September. Place in cool (45-50 degrees), dark place for about eight weeks so that a good root system will form. Then move to a sunny, warm, airy atmosphere. Feed biweekly after growth becomes active. Dry off after flowering and rest warm and dry from June to September.

PROPAGATION:

Remove offsets and pot separately in autumn.

Lantana

Cream, lavender, orange, pink, red, white, or yellow flowers all year.

CULTURE:

Nighttime temperature 50-60 degrees. Soil: equal parts garden loam, peat moss, and sand. Keep evenly moist and feed biweekly. Cut back as necessary to keep in bounds. White fly may necessitate spraying. Provide full sun in winter and plenty of daytime warmth in order to have winter bloom. An Ohio grower reports constant bloom in a 65-degree greenhouse.

PROPAGATION:

Make 3-inch cuttings from plants outdoors in September or October; root in moist vermiculite in warmth, humidity, and shade. Cuttings may be made also from February to April.

Lapeirousia

Crimson or red and yellow flowers January, February, and March.

CULTURE:

Nighttime temperature 45-50 degrees. This little relative of the iris requires freesia culture. Corms planted in fall may be placed immediately in a sunny, cool location. Keep evenly moist. The leaves are thin-textured and subject to tip browning in a hot, dry atmosphere. Feed biweekly after growth becomes active. Flowering continues over about a three-month period at a time when blooms are most appreciated. Seeds usually form, and if planted when dry, seedlings will yield some bloom the following year and an abundance the second season. Dry off in May or June and keep dormant until autumn.

PROPAGATION:

Remove offsets and pot separately in autumn.

Larkspur

Blue, pink, or white flowers February, March, April or May.

CULTURE:

Nighttime temperature 45-55 degrees. Grow in deep flats without transplanting, spacing about 6 x 6 inches. Provide full sun and cool, moist air. Discard after flowering.

PROPAGATION:

Sow seeds September, October, November, or December.

Lily

Fragrant flowers in many colors, late winter to early summer.

CULTURE:

Nighttime temperature 60 degrees. Pot dormant bulbs approximately five to six months before flowers are desired. After growth is up a few inches begin to feed biweekly with an evenly balanced (10-10-10, for example) liquid houseplant fertilizer. Keep in full sun. Provide fresh air on warm days. Buds just beginning to show one month before Easter will require 75-degree nighttime temperature in order to make the holiday. You can adjust the temperature up or down at this time in order to have blooms at Easter. After the flowers are gone, continue watering and feeding. Transplant to the garden as soon as the soil is warm and workable. Do not force the same bulbs again, at least not for several years.

Lobelia

Blue, rose-carmine, or white flowers April, May, and June.

CULTURE:

Nighttime temperature 60-65 degrees. Soil: equal parts garden loam, peat moss, and sand. Provide sunny, moist, airy

49 *Hybrid lilies like this Imperial Silver make spectacular flowering plants to grow in a home greenhouse. Plant the dormant bulbs in autumn or early winter for spring flowers.* OREGON BULB FARMS

atmosphere. Nice shelf plants close to the glass. Move outdoors in summer to baskets, boxes, pots, or directly into the garden for season-long color.

PROPAGATION:

Sow seeds from December to February for spring bloom.

Marguerite (*Chrysanthemum frutescens*)

Pink, white, or yellow flowers February to September. Supplemental lighting during short days of year (see "Asters, China") will increase the blooming season.

CULTURE:

Nighttime temperature 50-60 degrees. Start with young potted plants purchased from local commercial greenhouse or by mail. Soil: equal parts garden loam, peat moss, and sand. Keep evenly moist and feed biweekly. Provide full sun and moist, airy atmosphere. Marguerites summer nicely outdoors as container plants.

PROPAGATION:

Make 3-inch tip cuttings in April, May, June, or July. Root in moist vermiculite; provide shade and high humidity while roots form.

Marigold

Cream, orange, or yellow flowers from December to June.

CULTURE:

Nighttime temperature 50-60 degrees. Soil: two parts garden loam to one each of peat moss and sand. Keep evenly moist. Feed biweekly after plants are in final pots. Provide sunny, moist, airy atmosphere. Red-spider mite will be troublesome if air is hot, dry, and stale.

PROPAGATION:

Sow seeds in August or September for winter and spring bloom. Grow the French types in 3-inch pots. Transplant the American hybrids first to 3-inch pots, but before they become potbound, move to 6-inchers. At 60-degree nighttime temperature, 'Toreador' will bloom in about ninety days from seed; the Climax hybrids require one hundred days; all French types need one hundred and ten days.

Mignonette (*Reseda odorata*)

White and yellow fragrant flowers from November to spring.

CULTURE:

Nighttime temperature 45-50 degrees. Soil: equal parts garden loam, peat moss, and sand. Keep evenly moist and feed biweekly after growth is well-established. Provide sunny, moist, airy atmosphere.

PROPAGATION:

In June, July, or August, sow five or six seeds in each 3-inch pot of soil. After germination, remove all but the three strongest in each. Before these become rootbound, transplant to a 5-inch pot, but do not disturb the roots. When seedlings are about 3 inches tall, pinch out the growing tips to encourage branching.

Myosotis

Blue, forget-me-not flowers December to April. Plant 'Blue Bird' or 'Christmas Bouquet.'

CULTURE:

Nighttime temperature 45-55 degrees. Soil: equal parts garden loam, peat moss, and sand. Keep evenly moist. Feed biweekly from January to April. Discard at end of flowering season. Grow in sunny, cool, moist, airy atmosphere.

PROPAGATION:

Sow seeds in May, June, or July for bloom the following winter and spring season. Grow seedlings in a partially shaded, moist, cool location in summer. Transplant to 5- or 6-inch pots by October.

50 Myosotis, the much-loved forget-me-not, grows easily from seed to bloom in a home greenhouse that is sunny, airy, moist, and cool in the winter. AUTHOR

Narcissus

Creamy white or golden yellow fragrant flowers from December to March.

CULTURE:

Nighttime temperature 45-55 degrees. Soil: equal parts garden loam, peat moss, and sand. Pot bulbs in September or October, three to a 6-inch pot, more in a larger pot. Common paperwhites, the similar 'Soleil d'Or' (golden-yellow) and 'Cragford' (white with orange-scarlet crown) need only a short period of darkness and coolness after planting to form roots; two to six weeks at about 50 degrees. Then they may be brought to a sunny, warm, airy place for forcing. Daffodils like 'King Alfred,' 'Golden Harvest,' 'Trevithian,' and 'W. P. Milner' need at least eight to ten weeks of coolness (40-50 degrees) in nicely moist soil for the formation of a good root system. (A shelf in my unheated garage serves well as a convenient place for the root formation period.) Then pots may be brought into the greenhouse bench at two-week intervals for a succession of bloom. Miniatures like 'W. P. Milner' are good choices for a small greenhouse because they provide the welcome daffodil blooms in a minimum of space. After flowers wither, place the pots under the greenhouse bench, or in a frost-free coldframe, and when weather permits outdoors in spring, transplant to a permanent place in the garden. Do not force the same bulbs again. Discard paperwhites and similar types, unless you live in the deep South; there they may be naturalized in the outdoor garden.

Nasturtium

Orange, rose, scarlet, or yellow blooms from January to May. The Gleam hybrids are recommended for winter bloom. Try some of the new dwarf hybrids also. Nasturtiums are superb basket plants, close to the glass for full, baking sun.

CULTURE:

Nighttime temperature 50 degrees. Soil: two parts sand to one part each of peat moss and garden loam. Grow in sunny, airy atmosphere. Feed biweekly with a fertilizer low in nitrogen, 5-15-15, for example. Discard at end of flowering season.

PROPAGATION:

Sow seeds in August or September for winter blooms.

Nemesia

Blue, pink, red, rose, scarlet, orange, or yellow flowers February to May.

CULTURE:

Nighttime temperature 45-50 degrees. Soil: equal parts garden loam, peat moss, and sand. Keep on dry side and pinch once or twice during early stages of growth. This colorful annual resents hot nights, and therefore is not widely grown in this country. In a sunny, cool, airy greenhouse, it makes a beautiful spring-blooming plant that may be discarded at the beginning of summer heat.

PROPAGATION:

Sow seeds in August for February bloom on plants in 5-inch pots. Sow from October to December for bloom beginning in April from plants, three to an 8-inch pot.

Nerium

Rose, pink, purple, red, salmon-pink, or white flowers, primarily from May to August, but 'Mrs. Roeding' blooms intermittently all year. Known commonly as oleander.

CULTURE:

Nighttime temperature 45-55 degrees in winter, more at other times, although oleanders are not sensitive to changes.

51 Nerium, known otherwise as oleander, makes a beautiful, large flowering shrub or small tree in a home greenhouse. 'Mrs. Roeding,' the cultivar shown, has large, peach-pink flowers. AUTHOR

Soil: equal parts garden loam, peat moss, and sand. Keep evenly moist in spring and summer, a little less so in fall and winter. Feed biweekly in spring and summer. Provide full sun, and pot plant finally in a redwood tub as large as you can conveniently handle. Prune to shape in February, March, or April.

PROPAGATION:

Cuttings root easily in spring and summer, either in a glass of water, or in moist vermiculite. Sow seeds in spring or summer; seedlings will produce interesting variations, and first blooms may be expected the second season.

Nicotiana

Chartreuse, crimson, pink, or white flowers from January to June. The white *Nicotiana affinis* is fragrant at night. Known as flowering tobacco.

CULTURE:

Nighttime temperature 50-60 degrees. Soil: equal parts garden loam, peat moss, and sand. Plants in active growth need to be fed biweekly. Grow in sunny, moist, airy atmosphere. Spray carefully to control attacks of green aphids.

PROPAGATION:

Sow seeds in June, July, or August for bloom the following winter and spring. If you have nicotiana in the garden, old plants may be dug, cut back and potted in August or September for bloom beginning about January.

Nierembergia

Violet-blue or white flowers March, April, and May.

CULTURE:

Nighttime temperature 50 degrees. Soil: equal parts garden loam, peat moss, and sand. Keep evenly moist. Feed biweekly after plants start to bloom. This tender perennial may be kept through summer by shearing it back occasionally to give new strength. Before frost, cut back, repot, and place in sunny, airy position for winter.

PROPAGATION:

Sow seeds in December or January for spring bloom. February sowings will yield 3-inch blooming plants by May.

Orchids

The world of orchids is filled with an unequaled array of plants from which to choose for the flowering greenhouse. I am indebted to Joe S. Ritter of Clarksburg, West Virginia, who was willing to recommend from his large collection twelve orchids for all-year bloom in a home greenhouse:

January—Cattleya 'Bob Betts'
February—Phalaenopsis 'Texas Pink'
March—Cattleya 'Ave Maria'
April—*Cattleya skinneri*
May—Brassolaeliocattleya 'Ojai'
June—*Laeliocattleya canhamiana alba*
July—*Epidendrum tampense*
August—Cattleya 'Enid H.'
September— *Brassavola digbyana* var. *fimbripetala*
October—Cattleya 'Enid' alba
November—Cattleya 'Barbara Dane'
December—Cymbidium 'Fairy Wand'

To Mr. Ritter's select list, I recommend six other orchids for your consideration:

Brassavola nodosa (September-December)
Epidendrum fragrans (February-August)
Oncidium ampliatum majus (March-May)
O. splendidum (December-March)
O. tigrinum (December-January, freesia-scented)
Paphiopedilum maudiae (April-August)

CULTURE:

Nighttime temperature, as maintained in the Ritter greenhouse, 45 (ground level) to 65 (8 feet above ground); by day in winter the range is 58-75. Midsummer temperatures vary from 60 to 100 degrees. Cymbidiums need a cool to inter-

52 *Phalaenopsis is one of the easiest, most rewarding of all orchids to cultivate in a home greenhouse. Some have white flowers, others are subtle pastels.* WARD LINTON

mediate range; paphiopedilums and phalaenopsis need warmth; the other orchids listed will do well in nighttime temperatures of 50-70 degrees. Humidity: 60 per cent or more at all times. All the orchids listed require filtered sun, except the paphiopedilums and phalaenopsis which need shade. Grow cymbidiums and paphiopedilums in a mixture of four parts each of firbark, redwood fiber, and peat moss, to one of coarse sand; keep evenly moist. All the other orchids listed here may be cultivated in osmunda, or in medium coarse firbark that has been fortified with a small amount of leaf mold and perlite; drench with water, then allow to become dry before watering again.

The season and frequency of repotting varies from orchid to orchid. The best time to repot is usually when new root growth is just beginning. For many orchids, this occurs in the spring. Cymbidiums and paphiopedilums needn't be repotted more than once every two or three years. Repot *Brassavola nodosa* every year or two, but avoid disturbing *B. digbyana;* you can topdress it occasionally, first carefully removing some of the old growing medium. Repot oncidiums and phalaenopsis every two or three years, cattleyas and epidendrums every year or two. There are two general rules-of-thumb to follow in repotting an orchid: (1) Do so when the plant outgrows the pot, and (2) when the growing medium has broken down and is no longer in good condition.

PROPAGATION:

Most orchids have precise times when they are best divided, or when side shoots can be removed. I have propagated cane-stemmed epidendrums by air-layering. In a broad generalization, spring is the time to do this vegetative propagation. Growing orchids from seed is one of the amateur gardener's highest achievements. If you aspire to collecting orchids, I recommend membership in the American Orchid Society (Appendix).

Ornithogalum

White or yellow fragrant flowers in March. Select *O. arabicum, O. thyrsoides,* or *O.t. aureum.*

CULTURE:

Nighttime temperature 50-60 degrees. Soil: equal parts garden loam, peat moss, and sand. Pot three bulbs to a 6-inch pot in September or October. Keep in a cool (40-50 degrees), dark place for an eight-week rooting period. Then bring to sunny, warm, moist, and airy greenhouse location. Stake and tie as growth requires. Dry off after flowering as for freesias, and store dry until fall.

PROPAGATION:

Remove offsets at repotting time in autumn.

Osmanthus

White, fragrant flowers from January to June. Glossy, evergreen foliage.

CULTURE:

Nighttime temperature 50 degrees. Soil: equal parts garden loam, peat moss, and sand. Keep evenly moist. Feed biweekly during flowering period. Provide sun in winter, partial shade balance of the year. An outstanding permanent plant for a home greenhouse.

PROPAGATION:

Make 3-inch cuttings of firm, vigorous growth in May, June, or July. Insert in moist vermiculite; provide shade and high humidity. Always have young plants coming along to give your friends; this is a choice houseplant.

Oxalis

O. braziliensis, rosy red flowers from January to June; *O. melanosticta,* yellow flowers September to November; *O. ortgiesi,* everblooming, yellow flowers; *O. pes-caprae* (formerly *O. cernua*), yellow flowers from January to May; *O. regnelli,* white, nearly everblooming; and *O. rubra* (sometimes called *O. crassipes*), rose-pink, nearly everblooming.

CULTURE:

Nighttime temperature 45-60 degrees. Soil: equal parts garden loam, peat moss, and sand. Keep evenly moist and feed biweekly while in active growth. *O. braziliensis, O. melanosticta,* and *O. pes-caprae* need to be kept nearly dry for a resting period following the flowering season.

PROPAGATION:

Remove offsets or divide rhizomes at repotting time. Stem cuttings of *O. ortgiesi* root readily in moist vermiculite in a warm, shady, humid place.

53 *White-flowered* Oxalis regnelli *is nearly everblooming and one of the easiest of all plants to grow in a home greenhouse. Other species of oxalis have rose, pink, or yellow flowers.* AUTHOR

Pansy (*Viola tricolor*)

Flowers of almost every color from December to June.

CULTURE:

Nighttime temperature 40-50 degrees. Soil: equal parts garden loam, peat moss, and sand. Keep evenly moist. Feed biweekly from January on. Provide sunny, airy, moist, cool atmosphere.

PROPAGATION:

Sow seeds of the winter-blooming pansy from May to early August for winter and springtime bloom. Transplant seedlings first to small pots, later to a 5- or 6-inch size. This type pansy grows 3 to 4 feet tall and bears large flowers on stems 10 inches long; provide a string or wire trellis on which to train. Discard at end of flowering season.

Passiflora

The flowers of *P. alato-caerulea* are blue, pink, purple, and white. Those of *P. coccinea* are scarlet. Both are highly ornamental. Train the vines up a wall, then over the roof as natural shading. The flowers appear in spring and summer.

CULTURE:

Nighttime temperature 50-65 degrees. Soil: equal parts garden loam, peat moss, and sand. Keep evenly moist and feed biweekly. Provide trellis on which to climb. Grow in a large pot or tub.

PROPAGATION:

Take 4- to 6-inch cuttings from March to August; insert in moist vermiculite; provide high humidity and shade.

Pentas

Pink, rose, or white flowers all year.

CULTURE:

Nighttime temperature 50-65 degrees. Soil: equal parts garden loam, peat moss, and sand. Keep evenly moist. Fertilize biweekly. Provide full sun from October to April; partial shade from May to September. Cut back as necessary to keep in bounds.

PROPAGATION:

Make cuttings in April and root in moist vermiculite in high humidity at 70 degrees. These will be vigorous well-shaped plants for bloom the following winter.

54 *Scarlet passionflower,* Passiflora coccinea, *thrives under home greenhouse culture. It is a vine to train on a trellis, or along the walls and roof.* HENRY FIELD SEED & NURSERY COMPANY

55 *Fancy double ruffled petunia hybrids like 'Salmon Bouquet' are actually better performers in a home greenhouse in winter and late spring than they are outdoors in the summer garden. Start seeds in late autumn.* AUTHOR

Petunia

Blue, pink, purple, red, scarlet, white, or yellow flowers almost all year. Outstanding basket and shelf plants.

CULTURE:

Nighttime temperature 50-60 degrees. Soil: equal parts garden loam, peat moss, and sand. Keep evenly moist. Feed biweekly. Cut back after long flowering season.

PROPAGATION:

Sow seeds in June or July for young blooming plants from January on. Or, dig plants from garden in August or September. Cut back to 3 or 4 inches and vigorous new growth will follow. Stem cuttings may be rooted in July, August, or September for flowering plants beginning in January. Sow seeds of the fancy double grandifloras in December for blooms beginning in April.

Poinsettia

Cream, pink, or scarlet flowers December to February.

CULTURE:

Nighttime temperature 60-65 degrees. Soil: equal parts garden loam, peat moss, and sand. Keep evenly moist except nearly dry in March and April while plants rest under bench. In May move to warm, moist place and begin to water again.

56   Poinsettias like 'Eckespoint Standard' (shown) will fill a home greenhouse with red, pink, white, or marbled (two-colored) flowers from early December until spring. ECKE POINSETTIA RANCH

Feed September, October, November, and December for high quality blooms. Avoid drafts of cold or hot, dry air on poinsettias; they will lose foliage. Watch for infestations of mealybugs.

Poinsettias are short-day blooming plants. If a street light shines in your greenhouse, or you work in it at night in September, October, and November, so that plants do not have the normal period of darkness in every 24 hours, flowering may be delayed.

PROPAGATION:

Make 3- or 4-inch cuttings in May, June, July, or August. Cuttings rooted late should be potted three to five to a 6-inch pot in September. Root poinsettia cuttings in small pots of moist vermiculite or sphagnum moss in high humidity, warmth, and shade.

Primula

Blue, lavender, pink, rose, red, or yellow flowers from January to May. Three types are excellent for home greenhouses: *P. malacoides* (the fairy primrose), *P. obconica,* and *P. sinensis.* All are outstanding greenhouse plants.

CULTURE:

Nighttime temperature 45-65 degrees. Soil: equal parts garden loam, peat moss, leaf mold, and sand. Keep evenly moist. Provide a sunny, moist, airy atmosphere.

PROPAGATION:

Sow seeds of *P. malacoides* from April to August; *P. obconica* from March to June; and *P. sinensis* in March or April. Germinate at 60 degrees. Transplant to 2¼-inch pots, grouped in small flats to conserve moisture. Feed biweekly after they become established. Keep shaded and as cool as possible in summer. Before danger of freezing, move to greenhouse. Transplant to 5-inch pots by August or September, and finish in larger ones.

Punica

Orange-red, crepe-textured flowers from June to October. *P. granatum nana,* the dwarf pomegranate, makes an excellent permanent greenhouse plant.

CULTURE:

Nighttime temperature 45-60 degrees. In spring and summer provide full sun and warmth and abundant moisture; feed biweekly. In fall and winter keep in cool, airy, sunny location with soil on the dry side; do not feed. Cut back as necessary to keep a convenient size; this may be done whenever you have time to do it, usually from September to March. A good subject for bonsai work.

PROPAGATION:

Make cuttings of half-ripened wood in June or July; insert in moist vermiculite; provide shade and high humidity while roots are forming.

Ranunculus

Orange, pink, or yellow flowers in the spring.

CULTURE AND PROPAGATION:

The same as for anemone, which see.

Rose

Pink, red, white, or yellow fragrant flowers all year.

CULTURE:

Nighttime temperature 50-60 degrees. Obtain dormant bushes of hybrid teas or miniatures in November. Pot in 10- to 12-inch containers (the miniatures in 5- or 6-inch pots), using equal parts garden loam, peat moss, and sand. Place in airy, sunny location in the greenhouse. Keep evenly moist. Feed biweekly after new growth is evident. Spray or dust regularly to protect against powdery mildew, blackspot,

57 Hybrid tea, grandiflora, floribunda, and miniature roses grow easily as potted plants in a home greenhouse that is sunny, airy, and moist in the winter. JACKSON & PERKINS

and aphids. Summer outdoors, being sure the soil is always moist. Allow to freeze in autumn to induce dormancy; bring into greenhouse in December. Repot every year at this time.

Here are some roses I have enjoyed in my greenhouse: 'Baccara' (dark vermilion), 'Chrysler Imperial' (dark red, fragrant), 'Gail Borden' (pink and gold), 'Josephine Bruce' (crimson, fragrant), 'Mojave' (orange), 'Kordes Perfecta' (white, edged rosy pink), 'Gold Cup' (yellow, fragrant), and 'Vogue' (coral-red, fragrant).

Salpiglossis

Blue, lavender, purple, red, white or yellow trumpet-shaped flowers in April and May, on 2-foot plants.

CULTURE:

Nighttime temperature 50-65 degrees. Soil: equal parts garden loam, peat moss, and sand. Keep evenly moist. Feed biweekly from January until May. Provide sunny, airy, moist atmosphere in winter.

PROPAGATION:

Sow seeds in September or October for flowers the following April or May. Transplant 8 x 8 in deep bench by December, or grow three to a 10-inch pot. Stake and tie as necessary.

Salvia

The common flowering sage varieties, derived from *Salvia splendens,* yield pink, purple, salmon, or scarlet flowers from January to June. *S. rutilans,* the pineapple sage, has fragrant leaves and coral-red flowers from September to January.

CULTURE:

Nighttime temperature 50-60 degrees. Soil: equal parts garden loam, peat moss, and sand. Keep evenly moist. Feed biweekly. Provide sunny, airy, moist atmosphere.

PROPAGATION:

Sow seeds of *S. splendens* types in July, August, or September for vigorous flowering plants beginning the following January. Sow seeds in May or June to have fall-blooming specimens; these are especially handsome with chrysanthemums in the greenhouse. Cuttings of *S. rutilans* may be rooted at any time, but preferably in a warm, moist, humid, shaded place from March to July.

Schizanthus

Crimson, mauve, pink, purple, salmon, or red flowers from February to May.

CULTURE:

Nighttime temperature 45-60 degrees. Soil: equal parts garden loam, peat moss, and sand. Keep evenly moist in the early stages of growth; plantings kept on the dry side as they mature will yield earlier bloom. Begin to feed biweekly as soon as flower buds show. Provide a sunny, airy, moist atmosphere, not too warm at night. Discard after flowering.

PROPAGATION:

Sow seeds in August and September for flowers February to April. A January or February sowing will mature in May and June. Transplant first to 3-inch pots, finish in a 6- or 7-inch container. Pinch out the tips of seedlings once or twice to encourage branching.

Smithiantha

Rose, scarlet, or yellow flowers from June to February.

CULTURE:

Nighttime temperature 55-75 degrees. Soil: equal parts garden loam, peat moss, leaf mold, and sand. Keep evenly moist while in active growth; dry off after flowering and keep dormant at about 50 degrees until planting time. Provide sunny to partially shaded, warm, humid atmosphere. Feed biweekly from the time growth becomes active until buds show. This relative of the popular African violet and gloxinia grows from a scaly rhizome. Plant one to each 4-inch pot, or three to a 6-inch container; cover with about 1 inch of planting medium. Plant in June and July for winter bloom; February and March for summer; April or May for autumn.

PROPAGATION:

Divide rhizomes at repotting time. Sow seeds on surface of moist, milled sphagnum or vermiculite from March to June; keep warm (75-85 degrees), humid, and shaded.

58 *Snapdragons will produce flowers for greenhouse color or cutting all winter and spring. The variety shown is 'Madame Butterfly,' one of the showiest.* ALL-AMERICA SELECTIONS

Snapdragon (*Antirrhinum* species)

Bronze, lavender, pink, red, rose, white, or yellow flowers from November to June. For greenhouse forcing, these varieties are recommended: 'Afterglow' (golden-orange), 'Ball Lavender,' 'Cheviot Maid' (rose-pink), 'Cheviot Maid Yellow,' 'Coate's Yellow Perfection,' 'Dazzler' (scarlet), 'Jennie Schneider' (salmon-pink), 'Montana White,' 'Welcome' (crimson), and 'White Satin.'

CULTURE:

Nighttime temperature 45-60 degrees. Soil: equal parts garden loam, peat moss, and sand. Keep evenly moist. Feed monthly from September to December, biweekly beginning in January. Provide airy atmosphere and full sun. Spray as necessary to prevent aphid damage; or, try one of the new systematic insecticides on the soil. Discard plants at end of flowering season.

PROPAGATION:

Sow seeds in July for December bloom; in August for January to February. Generally, blooming begins about five months from seed sowing. Sow on surface of moist vermiculite or milled sphagnum moss, shade from direct sun, and keep at 70-75 degrees until seeds have germinated. Then move to a nighttime range of 50-60 degrees and provide full sun. When large enough to handle, transplant to 2¼-inch pots; move later to 5- or 6-inch pots or about 8 x 8 inches in a bench. You can grow single stem for earlier bloom, or pinch at 8-inch height to three good sets of leaves and thus obtain later but more bloom.

Solanum

Scarlet, cherrylike fruits from September to February. Not edible. The popular Jerusalem cherry.

CULTURE:

Nighttime temperature 45-65 degrees. Soil: equal parts garden loam, peat moss, and sand. Keep evenly moist. Feed biweekly. Provide sunny, airy, moist atmosphere in greenhouse. A tender perennial that may be trimmed in March, root-pruned, potted in fresh soil and saved year after year.

PROPAGATION:

Sow seeds from January to April, two to three to each 3-inch pot; keep warm (70-80 degrees), and moist. Later remove all but one seedling; this procedure saves transplanting. When first pot is filled with roots, transplant to 3-inch pot. Pinch or shear back two or three times to induce bushiness. Move outdoors from June to September. Feed biweekly and water abundantly. Spray flowers with water occasionally in daytime to encourage heavy fruit set. Do not allow soil to dry out severely at any time. Move back to greenhouse well ahead of cold weather.

Spathiphyllum

White spathes similar to the related anthurium and calla-lily, from March to November, above handsome dark green foliage.

CULTURE:

Nighttime temperature 65-70 degrees. Soil: equal parts garden loam, peat moss, leaf mold, and sand. Keep evenly moist and feed biweekly, except in autumn.

PROPAGATION:

Sow seeds in February or March; keep moist and warm (75-85 degrees). Divide well-established plants in February or March.

Stephanotis

Fragrant white flowers from March to June.

CULTURE:

Nighttime temperature 55-65 degrees. Soil: equal parts garden loam, peat moss, and sand. Keep evenly moist. Provide full sun in winter and spring; some shade in warm weather. Feed biweekly March to June. Cut back as necessary to keep in bounds after flowering season each year.

PROPAGATION:

Make cuttings of well-matured wood in March, April, or May; insert in moist vermiculite; provide warmth (65-75 degrees), humidity, and shade.

Stevia (*Piqueria trinervia*)

White, fragrant flowers from December to February.

CULTURE:

Nighttime temperature 45-55 degrees. Soil: equal parts garden loam, peat moss, and sand. Provide sunny, moist, airy atmosphere in fall and winter. Keep outdoors in summer. Be sure that soil stays evenly moist. Feed biweekly. Pinch out tips until September 1 to encourage branching.

PROPAGATION:

Sow seeds at 60-70 degrees in February. Take 3-inch cuttings in March, April, or May; root in moist vermiculite in shade and high humidity.

Stock (*Mathiola* species)

Pink, purple, rose, salmon, violet, or white fragrant flowers from January to May.

CULTURE:

Nighttime temperature 50-55 degrees. Soil: equal parts garden loam, peat moss, and sand. Feed biweekly from January through blooming season. Grow in full sun and in airy, cool, moist atmosphere. Flower buds form only when nighttime temperatures are below 60 degrees. Discard after flowering.

PROPAGATION:

Sow seeds in July or August for January bloom; October for March, April, and May.

Strelitzia

Orange and blue flowers intermittently from spring to fall.

CULTURE:

Nighttime temperature 55-65 degrees. Soil: equal parts garden loam, peat moss, and sand. Keep evenly moist, except on dry side from November to February. Feed biweekly from March to September. Provide full to partial sun and high humidity.

59 *Strelitzia or bird of paradise begins to flower after several years' growth in a 10-inch pot or tub when the roots have nearly filled the container. In the meantime it makes a handsome foliage plant.* WARD LINTON

PROPAGATION:

Divide large plants, but only if you have to, because re-establishment is a slow process, from February to April. Seeds require soaking in water for three or four days before sowing in moist peat moss and sand; keep warm (70-80 degrees); first bloom in seven years.

Streptosolen

Orange "browallia" flowers from January to June.

CULTURE:

Nighttime temperature 50-60 degrees. Soil: equal parts garden loam, peat moss, and sand; or grow in a basket of unmilled sphagnum moss. Keep evenly moist. Feed biweekly. Provide sunny, moist, airy atmosphere in the greenhouse. Cut back heavily after flowering.

PROPAGATION:

Make 3-inch tip cuttings from April to June. Root in moist vermiculite; provide high humidity and shade while roots are forming.

Sweet Alyssum

Lavender, pink, purple, or white flowers approximately 60 days following the sowing of seeds. An easily cultivated annual, excellent for edging benches, in pots and hanging baskets, and for fragrance.

CULTURE:

Nighttime temperature 45-65 degrees. Soil: equal parts garden loam, peat moss, and sand. Keep evenly moist. Feed biweekly. Provide sunny, moist, airy atmosphere. Long-blooming; shear back occasionally to encourage more flowers.

PROPAGATION:

Sow seeds in July or August for fall and winter bloom; sow December or January for spring.

Sweet Pea (*Lathyrus odoratus*)

All colors of fragrant flowers from November to June.

CULTURE:

Nighttime temperature 40-50 degrees. Soil: equal parts garden loam, peat moss, and sand. Keep evenly moist. Begin to feed biweekly as soon as plants are making attractive growth; use a low-nitrogen type such as 5-15-15. Provide string trellis on which the plants can climb; try also some of the new dwarf bush types like 'Bijou.' Grow sweet peas in seed flats at least 6 inches deep; or sow six to eight seeds in a 10-inch pot and allow about four to mature. Sweet peas need a sunny, airy, moist, cool atmosphere. Spraying may be necessary to control aphids.

PROPAGATION:

Sow seeds in July for November to February bloom; in August for December to March; in September for January to April; in October for February to May. A November sowing of winter-flowering varieties will yield April and May bloom. Plant Cuthbertsons in January for May and June bloom. Summer-started seedlings need to be kept as cool as possible; start them outdoors, but bring to the greenhouse well ahead of frost in autumn.

Tibouchina

Purple flowers March to October.

CULTURE:

Nighttime temperature 50-60 degrees. Soil: equal parts garden loam, peat moss, and sand. Keep evenly moist. Feed biweekly from March to October. Prune to shape in January or February.

PROPAGATION:

Make 3-inch tip cuttings of vigorous growth from February to June. Insert in moist vermiculite; provide warmth (70-80 degrees), high humidity, and shade. Pinch several times, but not after September, to encourage compact, bushy growth.

Tulbaghia

Lavender flowers intermittently all year on slender stems above narrow strap leaves. The flowers of *T. fragrans* are pleasingly fragrant. Foliage of the more common *T. violacea* or society garlic has a strong odor. Both plants are excellent subjects for a home greenhouse.

CULTURE:

Nighttime temperature 45-55 degrees. Soil: equal parts garden loam, peat moss, and sand. Provide full sun in fall, winter, and spring; some shade in summer. Keep evenly moist and feed biweekly.

PROPAGATION:

Divide well-established clumps any time.

Tulip

Orange, pink, red, white, or yellow flowers from late December to April. Single-flowered early varieties like 'Brilliant Star' (can be forced for Christmas), 'Diana,' 'Keizerskroon,' and 'Rose Luisante' are recommended; also the double-flowered earlies including 'Marechal Niel,' 'Murillo Maximus,' 'Peach Blossom,' 'Scarlet Cardinal,' and 'Schoonoord.'

CULTURE:

Nighttime temperature, after forcing begins, 45-55 degrees. Soil: equal parts garden loam, peat moss, and sand. Keep evenly moist. Plant five bulbs to each 6-inch pot (with flat side of bulb to outside of pot). Place in cool (35-45 degrees), dark place for a period of eight to twelve weeks for the formation of a good root system. During the time roots are forming, an unheated garage where temperatures do not dip below 32 degrees makes a convenient place so that pots can be kept clean easily, and the soil can be maintained in an evenly moist condition; also watch for signs of aphids. If these show, spray with mixture of houseplant pesticide following container directions. Any time afterwards begin forcing at 45-55 degrees in a sunny, airy, moist atmosphere.

After the flower petals drop, keep the foliage in good condition until the ground outdoors is workable. Then plant the tulips in a permanent place. Do not try to force the same bulbs again.

Ursinia

Orange daisy flowers from January to May.

CULTURE:

Nighttime temperature 45-55 degrees. Soil: equal parts garden loam, peat moss, and sand. Keep evenly moist. Feed biweekly from February until about May. Provide sunny, airy, moist atmosphere.

PROPAGATION:

Sow seeds in June or July for winter bloom. September or October sowings begin to bloom in March, and a January sowing will give May-June bloom. Plant three seedlings to a 5-inch pot.

Veltheimia

Dark pink, white, or yellow spikes of flowers from February to April, above rosettes of attractive foliage.

CULTURE:

Nighttime temperature 40-50 degrees, except 55-65 during the flowering season. Soil: equal parts garden loam, peat moss, and sand. Keep evenly moist, and feed biweekly, from October to June; keep nearly dry and do not feed from July to September. Repot every two or three years in August or September.

PROPAGATION:

Remove offsets at repotting time.

Zinnia

Salmon, scarlet, white, or yellow flowers from March to autumn. (To have earlier flowers, provide supplemental lighting as for "Asters, China," which see.)

CULTURE:

Nighttime temperature 55-65 degrees. Soil: equal parts garden loam, peat moss, and sand. Keep evenly moist. Feed biweekly after flowering is well along. Provide sunny, airy, warm atmosphere. 'Thumbelina,' an outstanding dwarf of recent introduction, is the only zinnia I recommend for a home greenhouse.

PROPAGATION:

Sow three or four seeds of 'Thumbelina' to each 5-inch bulb pan of soil in December or January for spring bloom. By this method, transplanting time is saved.

Appendix: *Lists for Ready Reference*

PLANTS FOR A COOL GREENHOUSE

(Nighttime minimum temperature 45-55 degrees **F**.)

Abutilon
Acacia
Agapanthus
Anemone
Aster, China
Azalea
Begonia, Hiemalis
  hybrids
Bellis
Browallia
Calceolaria
Calendula
Camellia
Campanula
Candytuft
Capsicum
Carnation
Centaurea
Chrysanthemum
Cineraria
Citrus
Clarkia
Clematis
Clivia
Coleus
Crocus
Cyclamen
Cyrtanthus
Daffodil
Didiscus

Dimorphotheca
Exacum
Felicia
Freesia
Gazania
Geranium
Gerbera
Gladiolus
Godetia
Gypsophila
Haemanthus
Herbs
Hibiscus, Chinese
Hyacinth
Hydrangea
Impatiens
Iris, Dutch
Ixia
Jasminum
Kalanchoe
Lachenalia
Lantana
Lapeirousia
Larkspur
Marguerite
Marigold
Mignonette
Myosotis
Narcissus
Nasturtium

Nemesia
Nerium
Nicotiana
Nierembergia
Ornithogalum
Osmanthus
Oxalis
Pansy
Passiflora
Pentas
Petunia
Primula
Punica
Ranunculus
Rose
Salpiglossis
Salvia
Schizanthus
Snapdragon
Solanum
Stevia
Stock
Streptosolen
Sweet Alyssum
Sweet Pea
Tibouchina
Tulbaghia
Tulip
Ursinia
Veltheimia

SAMPLE SCHEDULE FOR COOL GREENHOUSE

(Nighttime minimum temperature 45-55 degrees F.)

Name	Quantity for 10 x 10 Greenhouse	When to Start	Bloom Time
Abutilon	3	Cuttings in Sept.	All Year
Agapanthus	1	*	Spring or Summer
Begonia, Wax	12	Dec.-June or *	All Year
Begonia, Hiemalis hybrids	3	*	Fall-Winter
Camellia	3**	*	Oct.-April
Chrysanthemum	12	Cuttings in May	Aug.-Jan.
Cineraria	12	April-Sept.	Jan.-May
Clematis	12	* in Fall	Jan.-May
Cyclamen	12	July-Aug.	Nov.-April
Daffodil	50	Sept.-Oct.	Dec.-March
Freesia	100	Corms Aug.-Sept.	Dec.-March
Geranium (*Pelargonium hortorum* hybrids)	12	*	All Year
Hyacinth	12	Sept.-Oct.	Dec.-March
Nicotiana	3	May-June	Jan.-June
Schizanthus	25	Aug.-Sept.	Feb.-May
Snapdragon	25	July-Nov.	Dec.-June
Stock	25	July-Oct.	Jan.-May
Tulbaghia	3	*	All Year
Tulip	50	Oct.-Nov.	Dec.-April

* Obtain started plant(s) from commercial greenhouse
** Select early, midseason, and late varieties

PLANTS FOR MODERATE-TO-WARM GREENHOUSE

(Nighttime minimum temperature 55-70 degrees F.)

Acalypha	Azalea	Camellia
Achimenes	Begonia	Candytuft
African Violet	Beloperone	Capsicum
Agapanthus	Bougainvillea	Celosia
Ageratum	Bouvardia	Cestrum
Allamanda	Bromeliads	Chrysanthemum
Amaryllis	Browallia	Citrus
Anthurium	Cacti	Clematis
Aphelandra	Caladium	Clerodendrum
Ardisia	Calla-Lily	Clivia

PLANTS FOR MODERATE-TO-WARM GREENHOUSE

(Nighttime minimum temperature 55-70 degrees F.)

[Continued]

Coleus
Columnea
Crassula
Crossandra
Croton
Cyclamen
Cyrtanthus
Dimorphotheca
Dipladenia
Echeveria
Episcia
Euphorbia
Exacum
Felicia
Fuchsia
Gardenia
Gazania
Geranium
Gerbera
Gladiolus
Gloriosa
Haemanthus
Heliotrope

Herbs
Hibiscus, Chinese
Hoya
Hyacinth
Hydrangea
Impatiens
Ixia
Ixora
Jacobinia
Jasminum
Kaempferia
Kalanchoe
Lantana
Lapeirousia
Lily
Lobelia
Marguerite
Marigold
Nicotiana
Orchids
Ornithogalum
Oxalis
Passiflora

Pentas
Petunia
Poinsettia
Primula
Punica
Rose
Salpiglossis
Salvia
Schizanthus
Smithiantha
Snapdragon
Solanum
Spathiphyllum
Stephanotis
Strelitzia
Sweet Alyssum
Tibouchina
Tulbaghia
Zinnia

SAMPLE SCHEDULE FOR MODERATE-TO-WARM GREENHOUSE

(Nighttime minimum temperature 55-70 degrees F.)

Name	Quantity for 10 x 10 Greenhouse	When to Start	Bloom Time
Achimenes	50	Rhizomes Feb.-April	June-Oct.
African violet	12	*	All Year
Amaryllis	12	Fall-Winter *	Nov.-May
Begonia, Wax	12	Dec.-June or *	All Year
Begonia, Angelwing	3	*	All Year
Beloperone	1	*	All Year
Bougainvillea 'Barbara Karst'	1	*	Fall-Spring

* Obtain started plant(s) from commercial greenhouse

SAMPLE SCHEDULE FOR MODERATE-TO-WARM GREENHOUSE

(Nighttime minimum temperature 55-70 degrees F.)

[*Continued*]

Citrus	3	*	All Year
Clivia	1	*	March-June
Cyrtanthus	3	Bulbs Aug.-Oct.	Nov.-Jan.
Fuchsia 'Gartenmeister Bohnstedt'	1	*	All Year
Epidendrum orchids	3	*	All Year
Geranium (*Pelargonium hortorum* hybrids)	12	*	All Year
Gloxinia	50	Tubers Feb.-April	May-Sept.
Hibiscus, Chinese	6	*	All Year
Impatiens	12	Dec.-June	All Year
Kalanchoe blossfeldiana	12	Seeds Jan.-July	Jan.-May
Marigold 'Toreador'	6	Aug.-Sept.	Dec.-June
Nicotiana	3	June-Aug.	Jan.-June
Petunia	12	May-June, or dig from garden in Sept.	All Year
Poinsettia	3	* or cuttings May-Aug.	Dec.-Feb.

* Obtain started plant(s) from commercial greenhouse

EVERBLOOMING GREENHOUSE PLANTS

(Those that flower intermittently all year are followed by "i.")

Abutilon	Geranium
African Violet	Hibiscus, Chinese
Begonia	Impatiens
Beloperone	Ixora (i)
Bougainvillea (i)	Jacobinia (i)
Citrus (i)	Lantana
Columnea	Nerium 'Mrs. Roeding' (i)
Crossandra	Pentas
Episcia	Petunia
Euphorbia Splendens	Rose (i)
Fuchsia	Tulbaghia (i)

PERIODICALS ABOUT GREENHOUSE PLANTS

African Violet Magazine, bi-monthly publication of the African Violet Society of America, Inc., Box 1326, Knoxville, Tennessee 37901.

American Fern Journal, quarterly publication of the American Fern Society, Biological Sciences Group, University of Connecticut, Storrs, Connecticut 06268.

American Ivy Society Bulletin, periodical of the American Ivy Society, 128 West 58th Street, New York, New York 10019.

American Orchid Society Bulletin, monthly publication of the American Orchid Society, Inc., Botanical Museum of Harvard University, Cambridge, Massachusetts 02138.

The Begonian, monthly of the American Begonia Society, Inc., 139 North Ledoux Road, Beverly Hills, California 90211.

Bonsai (quarterly) and *ABStracts* (monthly newsletter), publications of the American Bonsai Society, 953 South Shore Drive, Lake Waukomis, Parksville, Missouri 64151.

Bonsai Magazine, ten-times-a-year publication of Bonsai Clubs International, 445 Blake Street, Menlo Park, California 94025.

The Bromeliad Journal, bi-monthly publication of the Bromeliad Society, Inc., P.O. Box 3279, Santa Monica, California 90403.

Cactus and Succulent Journal, bi-monthly publication of the Cactus and Succulent Society of America, Inc., Box 167, Reseda, California 91335.

The Camellia Journal, quarterly publication of the American Camellia Society, Box 212, Fort Valley, Georgia 31030.

Cymbidium Society News, monthly publication of the Cymbidium Society of America, Inc., 6787 Worsham Drive, Whittier, California 90602.

Epiphyllum Bulletin, publication of the Epiphyllum Society of America, 218 East Greystone Avenue, Monrovia, California 91016.

Geraniums Around the World, quarterly publication of the International Geranium Society, 11960 Pascal Avenue, Colton, California 92324.

Gesneriad Saintpaulia News, bi-monthly publication of the American Gesneria Society, 11983 Darlington Avenue, Los Angeles, California 90049.

Gesneriad Saintpaulia News, bi-monthly publication of Saintpaulia International, P.O. Box 10604, Knoxville, Tennessee 37919.

The Gloxinian, bi-monthly publication of the American Gloxinia and Gesneriad Society, Inc., P.O. Box 174, New Milford, Connecticut 06776.

Hobby Greenhouse Owner's Association of America, Box 674, Corte Madera, California 94925.

Light Garden, bi-monthly publication of the Indoor Light Gardening Society of America, Inc., 128 West 58th Street, New York, New York 10019.

Monthly Fern Lessons, with newsletter and annual magazine, publications of the Los Angeles International Fern Society, 2423 Burritt Avenue, Redondo Beach, California 90278.

The National Fuchsia Fan, monthly publication of the National Fuchsia Society, 10934 East Flory Street, Whittier, California 90606.

The Orchid Digest, 25 Ash Avenue, Corte Madera, California 94925.

Plantlife-Amaryllis Yearbook, bulletin of the American Plant Life Society, Box 150, La Jolla, California 92037.

Plants Alive, monthly magazine about indoor gardening, 1255 Portland Place, Boulder, Colorado 80302.

Popular Gardening Indoors, 383 Madison Avenue, New York, New York 10017.

Princepes, quarterly publication of the Palm Society, 1320 South Venetian Way, Miami, Florida 33139.

Seed Pod, quarterly publication of the American Hibiscus Society, Box 98, Eagle Lake, Florida 33139

Terrarium Topics, published by The Terrarium Association, 57 Wolfpit Avenue, Norwalk, Connecticut 06851

Under Glass, bi-monthly devoted to home greenhouse growing; c/o Lord & Burnham, Irvington, New York 10533.

SOURCES FOR GREENHOUSES, SUPPLIES, AND PLANTS

Abbey Garden, 176 Toro Canyon Road, Carpinteria, California 93013. Complete listing of cacti and other succulents; catalog 50¢.

Abbot's Nursery, Route 4, Box 482, Mobile, Alabama 36609. Camellias.

Acme Engineering Corporation, P.O. Box 978, Muskogee, Oklahoma 74401. Prefabricated greenhouses.

Alberts & Merkel Bros., Inc. 2210 S. Federal Highway, Boynton Beach, Florida 33435. Orchids, plus an amazing array of tropical foliage and flowering houseplants; send 25¢ for list.

Alenco, P.O. Box 3309, Bryan, Texas 77801. Window greenhouses.

Aluminum Greenhouses, Inc., 14615 Lorain Avenue, Cleveland, Ohio 44111. Prefabricated home greenhouses.

Antonelli Bros., 2545 Capitola Road, Santa Cruz, California 95060. Tuberous begonias, gloxinias, achimenes.

Louise Barnaby, 12178 Highview Street, Vicksburg, Michigan 49097. African violets; send stamp for list.

Mrs. Mary V. Boose, 9 Turney Place, Trumbull, Connecticut 06611. African violets and episcias; 15¢ for list.

John Brudy's Rare Plant House, P.O. Box 1348, Cocoa Beach, Florida 32931. Unusual seeds and plants; catalog $1.

Buell's Greenhouses, Weeks Road, Eastford, Connecticut 06242. Complete listing of gloxinias, African violets and other gesneriads; send $1.00 for catalog.

Burgess Seed & Plant Co., 67 East Battle Creek, Galesburg, Michigan 49053. Houseplants and bulbs.

W. Atlee Burpee Co., Warminster, Pennsylvania 18974. Seeds, bulbs, supplies and equipment for indoor gardening; prefabicated home greenhouses.

David Buttram, P.O. Box 193, Independence, Missouri 64051. African violets; send 10¢ for list.

Cactus Gem Nursery, 10092 Mann Drive, Cupertino, California (visit Thursday-Sunday); by mail write P.O. Box 327, Aromas, California 95004.

Casaplanta, 16129 Cohasset Street, Van Nuys, California 91406. Prefabricated, portable home greenhouses.

Castle Violets, 614 Castle Road, Colorado Springs, Colorado 80904. African violets.

Champion's African Violets, 8848 Van Hoesen Road, Clay, New York 13041. African violets; send stamp for list.

Christen, Inc., 59 Branch St., St. Louis, Missouri 63147. Wood benches, tables and risers for home greenhouses and plant rooms.

Victor Constantinov, 3321 21st Street, Apt. 7, San Francisco, California 94110. African violets; columneas and episceas; send stamp for list.

Cook's Geranium Nursery, 714 N. Grand, Lyons, Kansas 67544. Geraniums; send 25¢ for catalog.

Davis Cactus Garden, 1522 Jefferson Street, Kerrville, Texas 78028. Send 25¢ for catalog.

P. de Jager and Sons, 188 Asbury Street, South Hamilton, Massachusetts 01982. Bulbs for forcing as well as others for the greenhouse.

L. Easterbrook Greenhouses, 10 Craig Street, Butler, Ohio 44822. African violets, other gesneriads, terrarium plants and supplies; complete catalog 75¢.

Eden Greenhouses, 546 W. Broadway, Cedarhurst, New York 11516. Prefabricated greenhouses.

Electric Farm, 104 B Lee Road, Oak Hill, New York 12460. Gesneriads; send self-addressed stamped envelope for free list.

Environmental Dynamics, Box 996, Sunnymead, California 92388. Greenhouses and accessories.

Farmer Seed and Nursery Co., Faribault, Minnesota 55021. Houseplants.

Fennell Orchid Co., Inc., 26715 SW. 157th Avenue, Homestead, Florida 33030.

Fernwood Plants, 1311 Fernwood Pacific Drive, Topanga, California 90290. Rare and unusual cacti.

Ffoulkes, 610 Bryan Street, Jacksonville, Florida 32202. African violets; send 25¢ for list.

Henry Field Seed & Nursery Co., 407 Sycamore, Shenandoah, Iowa 51601. Houseplants; supplies.

Fischer Greenhouses, Linwood, New Jersey 08221. African violets and other gesneriads; send 25¢ for catalog.

Floralite Co., 4124 E. Oakwood Road, Oak Creek, Wisconsin 53154. Fluorescent-light gardening equipment and supplies.

Four Seasons Greenhouse Co., 17 Ave. of the Americas, New York, New York 10013. Prefabricated greenhouses.

Fox Orchids, 6615 W. Markham, Little Rock, Arkansas 72205. Orchids and supplies for growing them at home.

Arthur Freed Orchids, Inc., 5731 S. Bonsall Drive, Malibu, California 90265. Orchids and supplies for growing them at home.

J. Howard French, Baltimore Pike, Lima, Pennsylvania 19060. Bulbs for forcing.

Garden of Eden Greenhouse Center, 875 E. Jericho Turnpike, Huntington Station, New York 11746. Prefabricated home greenhouses.

Gothic Arch Greenhouses, P.O. Box 1564, Mobile, Alabama 36601. Prefabricated greenhouses.

The Greenhouse, 9515 Flower Street, Bellflower, California 90706. Fluorescent-light gardening equipment.

Greenhouse Specialties, 9849 Kimker Lane, St. Louis, Missouri 63127. Prefabricated home greenhouses and accessories; catalog $1.

Grigsby Cactus Gardens, 2354 Bella Vista Drive, Vista, California 92083. Catalog 50¢.

Gurney Seed and Nursery Co., Yankton, South Dakota 57078. Houseplants.

Orchids by Hausermann, Inc., P.O. Box 363, Elmhurst, Illinois 60126. Complete array of orchids and supplies for growing them; catalog $1.25.

Helen's Cactus, 2205 Mirasol, Brownsville, Texas 78520. Send stamp for list.

Henrietta's Nursery, 1345 N. Brawley Avenue, Fresno, California 93705. Cacti/succulents; catalog 20¢.

Hilltop Farm, Route 3, Box 216, Cleveland, Texas. Geraniums and herbs.

Sim T. Holmes, 100 Tustarawas Road, Beaver, Pennsylvania 15009. African violets, miniature and regular; all grown under fluorescent light.

The House of Violets, 936 Garland Street. S.W., Camden, Arkansas 71701. Self-watering African-violet planters.

House Plant Corner, Box 5000, Cambridge, Maryland 21613. Supplies and equipment for growing houseplants; send 20¢ for catalog.

Spencer M. Howard Orchid Imports, 11802 Huston Street, North Hollywood, California 91607. Species and unusual orchids; free list.

Gordon M. Hoyt Orchids, Seattle Heights, Washington 98036. Complete listing of interesting orchids for the home grower.

Hydroponic Chemical Co., Copley, Ohio 44321. Special houseplant fertilizers.

Margaret Ilgenfritz Orchids, Blossom Lane, P.O. Box 665, Monroe, Michigan. Catalog $1.

Indoor Gardening Supplies, P.O. Box 40551, Detroit, Michigan 48240. Fluorescent-light gardening equipment.

Jackson & Perkins, Medford, Oregon 97501. Hybrid roses.

Jones and Scully, 2200 N.W. 33rd Avenue, Miami, Florida 33142. Remarkable catalog of orchids and supplies for growing them at home; $3.50 per copy.

Kartuz Greenhouses, 92 Chestnut Street, Wilmington, Massachusetts 01887. Begonias, gesneriads, houseplants; catalog 50¢.

Wm. Kirch—Orchids, Ltd., 2630 Waiomao Road, Honolulu, Hawaii 96816. Orchids.

Kirkpatrick's, 27785 De Anza Street, Barstow, California 92311. Cacti/succulents; send stamp for list.

Kolb's Greenhouses, 725 Belvidere Road, Phillipsburg, New Jersey 08865. African violets; send stamp for list.

Lauray, Undermountain Road, Route 41, Salisbury, Connecticut 06068. Gesneriads, cacti/succulents, begonias; send 50¢ for catalog.

Logee's Greenhouses, 55 North Street, Danielson, Connecticut 06239. Complete selection of houseplants; catalog $1.

Lord and Burnham, Irvington, New York 10533. Home greenhouses.

Lyndon Lyon, 14 Mutchler Street, Dolgeville, New York 13329. African violets and other gesneriads.

Mary's African Violets, 19788 San Juan, Detroit, Michigan 48221. Supplies and lighting equipment.

Earl May Seed & Nursery Co., Shenandoah, Iowa 51603. Houseplants.

McGregor Greenhouses, Box 36, Santa Cruz, California 95063. Prefabricated greenhouses and accessories.

Rod McLellan Co., 1450 El Camino Real, S. San Francisco, California 94080. Orchids and supplies for growing them at home.

Merry Gardens, Camden, Maine 04843. Houseplants and herbs; catalog $1.

Mini-Roses, P.O. Box 245, Station A., Dallas, Texas 75208. Miniature roses.

Modlin's Cactus Gardens, Route 4, Box 3034, Vista, California 92083. Catalog 25¢.

Cactus by Mueller, 10411 Rosedale Highway, Bakersfield, California 93308. 10¢ for list.

National Greenhouse Company, P.O. Box 100, Pana, Illinois 62557. Prefabricated greenhouses and accessories.

Nature's Way Products, 3505 Mozart Avenue, Cincinnati, Ohio 45211. Perlite, other soil conditioners, fertilizer, potting soils; send stamp for list.

J. A. Nearing Co., 10788 Tucker Street, Beltsville, Maryland 20705. Prefabricated home greenhouses.

Walter F. Nicke, Hudson, New York. Useful as well as unusual gardening supplies and equipment, much of it made in England.

Nuccio's Nurseries, 3555 Chaney Trail, Altadena, California 91001. Hybrid camellias and azaleas.

Orinda Nursery, Bridgeville, Delaware 19933. Hybrid camellias.

George W. Park Seed Co., Inc., Greenwood, South Carolina 29647. Seeds, bulbs, fluorescent-light gardening supplies and equipment; very large, complete catalog, free for the asking.

Penn Valley Orchids, 239 Old Gulph Road, Wynnewood, Pennsylvania. Peters fertilizers, available in several formulations designed for specific growth responses.

Ra-Pid-Gro Corp., 88° Ossian, Dansville, New York 14437. Manufacturers of Ra-Pid-Gro fertilizer.

Redfern's Prefab Greenhouses, 55 Mount Hermon Road, Scotts Valley, California 95066.

Redwood Domes, P.O. Box 666, Aptos, California 95003. Prefabricated home greenhouses.

Peter Reimuller, 980 17th Avenue, Santa Cruz, California 95063. Prefabricated home greenhouses.

John Scheepers, Inc., 63 Wall Street, New York, New York 10005. Specialists in flowering bulbs.

Schmelling's African Violets, 5133 Peck Hill Road, Jamesville, New York 13078. African violets; catalog 20¢.

Sequoia Nursery, 2519 E. Noble, Visalia, California 93277. Miniature roses.

Shaffer's Tropical Gardens, Inc., 1220 41 Avenue, Capitola, California 95010. Orchids.

P. R. Sharp, 104 N. Chapel Avenue, #3, Alhambra, California 91801. South American and Mexican cacti.

Shoplite Co., Inc., 566 Franklin Avenue, Nutley, New Jersey 07110. Fluorescent-light gardening equipment; catalog 25¢.

R. H. Shumway, Seedsman, Rockford, Illinois 61101. Houseplants and bulbs.

Singers' Growing Things, 6385 Enfield Avenue, Reseda, California 91335. Succulents.

Smith's Cactus Garden, P.O. Box 871, Paramount, California 90723. Send 30¢ for list.

Star Roses, Box 203, West Grove, Pennsylvania 19390, Miniature and other roses.

Fred A. Stewart, Inc., Orchids, 1212 E. Las Tunas Drive, San Gabriel, California 91778. Orchids.

Ed Storms, 4223 Pershing, Fort Worth, Texas 76107. Lithops and other succulents.

Sturdi-built Manufacturing Co., 11304 S.W. Boones Ferry

Road, Portland, Oregon 97219. Prefabricated home greenhouses.

Sunnybrook Farms, 9448 Mayfield Road, Chesterland, Ohio 44026. Herbs; scented geraniums; *Aloe vera,* the "Unguentine plant."

Sure Crop, Inc., 167 Cranston Court, Glen Ellyn, Illinois 60137. Window greenhouses.

Texas Greenhouse Co., Inc., 2717 St. Louis Avenue, Fort Worth, Texas 76110. Prefabricated home greenhouses.

Thompson & Morgan, Inc., P.O. Box 24, Somerdale, New Jersey 08083. Many unusual houseplant seeds.

Tinari Greenhouses, Box 190, 2325 Valley Road, Huntington Valley, Pennsylvania 19006. African violets, gesneriads, supplies and equipment; catalog 25¢.

Tube Craft, Inc., 1311 W. 80th Street, Cleveland, Ohio 44102. Fluorescent-light gardening equipment.

Turner Greenhouses, P.O. Box 117, Goldsboro, North Carolina 27530. Prefabricated home greenhouses.

Vegetable Factory, Inc., 100 Court Street, Copiague, New York 11726. Prefabricated home greenhouses.

Volkmann Bros. Greenhouses, 2714 Minert Street, Dallas, Texas 75219. Send stamped, self-addressed long envelope for catalog of African violets and supplies, including the Reservoir Wick Pot.

Werth's, P.O. Box 1902, Cedar Rapids, Iowa 52406. Plans for plastic-covered home greenhouse; $3.

Wheeling Corrugating Co., Wheeling, West Virginia 26003. Prefabricated home greenhouses.

Wilson Brothers, Roachdale, Indiana 47121. Houseplants; many geraniums.

H. E. Wise, 3710 June Street, San Bernardino, California 92405. Cacti; send stamp for list.

Mrs. Ernie Wurster, Route 1, Box 156, Elizabeth, Illinois 61028. African violets; send 15¢ for list.

INDEX

Index

Italic numbers refer to pages on which there are illustrations.

SIGNET Books You'll Want to Read

☐ **CONSUMER GUIDE®: HOW IT WORKS & HOW TO FIX IT.** Clear, expert explanations of how products work and what to do when they break down. Written in precise, non-technical language and illustrated with schematic drawings to simplify many home repair projects. (#E8874—$2.50)

☐ **CONSUMER GUIDE: COMPLETE GUIDE TO USED CARS.** Auto experts rate the best used car buys from 1969 to 1978. Performance test reports, recall records, mileage ratings and price range charts help you make the right choice in a used car from General Motors, Ford, Chrysler, AMC and foreign manufacturers. (#E8672—$2.50)

☐ **HOYLE'S RULES OF GAMES (revised) by Albert H. Morehead and Geoffrey Mott-Smith.** Authoritative rules and instructions for playing hundreds of indoor games. New bridge bidding and scoring rules. (#E9001—$2.25)

☐ **THE SIGNET BOOK OF WINE by Alexis Bespaloff.** Everything you need to know about wine from the noblest vintages to the everyday vins ordinaire. Over 500 wines from eighteen countries are described. Contains maps, ratings of recent vintage years, a pronunciation guide, a comprehensive index and advice on how to start your own wine cellar. (#J8208—$1.95)

☐ **THE SIGNET BOOK OF AMERICAN WINE by Peter Quimme.** Complete, authoritative and practical, everything you need to know to buy, evaluate, and enjoy all the different wines of America. The indispensable companion volume to THE SIGNET BOOK OF WINE. (#J7653—$1.95)

Buy them at your local

bookstore or use coupon on

next page for ordering.

SIGNET Books for Your Reference Shelf

☐ **THE NEW AMERICAN MEDICAL DICTIONARY AND HEALTH MANUAL by Robert E. Rothenberg, M.D., F.A.C.S.** This newly revised third edition includes a complete Medicare Handbook and up-to-date information on contraceptive drugs and devices in addition to over 8700 definitions of medical terms, diseases and disorders, a comprehensive health manual, charts and tables and much, much more. With over 300 illustrations. (#E8314—$2.50)

☐ **CALORIES AND CARBOHYDRATES by Barbara Kraus.** Foreword by Edward B. Greenspan, M.D. Revised Edition. This dictionary contains 8,000 brand names and basic foods with their caloric and carbohydrate counts. Recommended by doctors, nutritionists, and family food planners as an indispensable aid to those who must be concerned with what they eat, it will become the most important diet reference source you will ever own. (#E8544—$2.50)

☐ **HOW TO KNOW THE BIRDS by Roger Tory Peterson.** In this compact handbook, a noted ornithologist and artist describes over 200 species of birds, including flying style, body outline, field markings, habits, peculiarities and legends. 72 color illustrations and over 400 black-and-white drawings. (#W7481—$1.50)

☐ **HOW TO KNOW AMERICAN ANTIQUES by Alice Winchester.** How to recognize American antiques such as silver, furniture, pewter, china and needlework. Over 300 drawings. (#W7600—$1.50)

More SIGNET Books of Interest

☐ **CONSUMER GUIDE: RATING & RAISING INDOOR PLANTS by Virginia L. Beatty and the Editors of Consumer Guide.** A practical guide for successful indoor gardening—including handy lists of the best hanging plants, floor plants, plants for dry apartments, and hundreds of pictures for easy identification. (#E7160—$2.25)

☐ **THE SUPERMARKET HANDBOOK Access to Whole Foods by Nikki and David Goldbeck.** This book will prove invaluable to any shopper concerned with the quality and nutritive value of foods available in today's supermarkets. It will help you to understand labels and select foods with a discerning eye, and provides easy, low-cost ways of preparing and using whole foods to replace processed foods. "An enormously useful and heartening work!"—*The New York Times* (#E8106—$2.25)

☐ **THE LOS ANGELES TIMES NATURAL FOODS COOKBOOK by Jeanne Voltz, Food Editor, Woman's Day Magazine.** Discover the joys of cooking and eating naturally with this book of over 600 savory, simple-to-follow recipes. Whether you are concerned with taste or nutrition, these delicious and healthy recipes—high in fiber content—will delight everyone from the gourmet chef to the dedicated dieter. (#E9038—$2.95)

☐ **THE SOUP-TO-DESSERT HIGH-FIBER COOKBOOK by Betty Wason.** The important new high-fiber, low-calorie diet that adds flavor and good health to every meal you eat! Low-calorie menus, hundreds of delicious recipes, food composition charts and a fiber diet dictionary make this book an absolutely essential kitchen companion for every cook who cares about good health and good eating. (#J7208—$1.95)

Buy them at your local

bookstore or use coupon on

next page for ordering.